WORKBOOK

HOW
PEOPLE
GROW

Resources by Henry Cloud and John Townsend

Boundaries
Boundaries Workbook
Boundaries Audio Pages®
Boundaries video curriculum
Boundaries in Dating
Boundaries in Dating Workbook
Boundaries in Dating Audio Pages®
Boundaries in Dating curriculum
Boundaries in Marriage
Boundaries in Marriage Workbook
Boundaries in Marriage Audio Pages®
Boundaries with Kids
Boundaries with Kids Workbook
Boundaries with Kids Audio Pages®
Changes That Heal (Cloud)
Changes That Heal Workbook (Cloud)
Changes That Heal Audio Pages® (Cloud)
Hiding from Love (Townsend)
How People Grow
How People Grow Workbook
How People Grow Audio Pages®
The Mom Factor
The Mom Factor Workbook
The Mom Factor Audio Pages®
Raising Great Kids
Raising Great Kids for Parents of Preschoolers curriculum
Raising Great Kids Workbook for Parents of Preschoolers
Raising Great Kids Workbook for Parents of School-Age Children
Raising Great Kids Workbook for Parents of Teenagers
Raising Great Kids Audio Pages®
Safe People
Safe People Workbook
Safe People Audio Pages®
Twelve "Christian" Beliefs That Can Drive You Crazy

WORKBOOK

HOW PEOPLE GROW

What the Bible Reveals about Personal Growth

DR. HENRY CLOUD
DR. JOHN TOWNSEND

with Lisa Guest

GRAND RAPIDS, MICHIGAN 49530 USA

ZONDERVAN™

How People Grow Workbook

Copyright © 2002 by Henry Cloud and John Townsend

Requests for information should be addressed to:

Zondervan, *Grand Rapids, Michigan 49530*

ISBN: 0-310-24569-9

Published in association with Yates & Yates, LLP, Attorneys and Counselors, Suite 1000, Literary Agent, Orange, CA.

Interior design by Susan Ambs

Printed in the United States of America

02 03 04 05 06 07 08 /❖ DC/ 10 9 8 7 6 5 4 3 2 1

CONTENTS

PART FOUR
The Path of Growth

Welcome to the How People Grow Workbook

We hope that the time you invest in these pages will bring you closer to God and to his paths of growth in your life. Let us briefly orient you to the design of this workbook so that you can maximize its benefits. We have written this workbook as a companion to our book *How People Grow*. It contains excerpts from and references to that book; stimulating questions to help you make personal observations, apply them to your own life, and explore new challenges in your own individual journey; prayers to help you depend on God for your growth; and tips for growth in separate sidebars. A lot of questions in this workbook will prompt you to reflect on your own life — both past and present. If you have not had the experience being referred to in the question, just skip the question, but be honest!

The workbook has been constructed to follow the principles of *How People Grow*. We hope you will discover that doctrine and theology are not boring intellectual exercises, but exciting living revelations of a God who brings you back to life in all areas.

What we have tried to do in this workbook is to help you make the growth process work in your life. You will find opportunity to get to know God and Jesus, and to connect with the Holy Spirit. You will be asked to connect with others, tell the truth about life and yourself, and face some difficult challenges. You will have the opportunity to take new risks and work through old patterns. You will be encouraged that others are on the same path. We hope that you will see God not as someone religious, but as the one who wants to bring his life and principles into your everyday life. And, in the process, we hope that theology and the Bible become very practical life-giving realities for you.

In addition, we would encourage you to study this material in a group if at all possible. When people who desire growth get together, good things happen. They share successes and failures, and they encourage one another. We hope that the workbook will be a vehicle not only for your growth, but also for your deeper connections with God and the people in your group.

We would suggest a structured approach to this material. Doing the assignments and meeting regularly can be a meaningful step on your path of growth. It is not meant to restrict you, but rather to make growth a daily part of your thought life, prayer life, and emotional life.

We wish you God's best, and we hope that his grace will support, encourage, and transform all parts of your life.

SINCERELY,

HENRY CLOUD, PH.D.

JOHN TOWNSEND, PH.D.

PART ONE

Paradise Lost

CHAPTER ONE

Harder Than I Thought

It was my (Henry's) first day on the job in a Christian psychiatric hospital. I was all geared up to teach the patients how to find the life I knew awaited them as soon as they learned the truth I had been taught. I was thinking all I had to do was tell people God loved them, and if they would understand more of what he has said, they would be well.

Then a woman in a pink bathrobe walked out of her room, extended her arms outward, and exclaimed, "I am Mary, Mother of God!"

Suddenly I was shaken into reality. *This is going to be harder than I thought,* I realized. It was a thought I would have many times in the years to come.

FOUR MODELS OF HOW PEOPLE GROW (Page 16)*

In Christian circles at the time I was beginning my training, there were basically four popular ways of thinking about personal growth.

The sin model: All problems are a result of one's sin.

The truth model: The truth of the Bible will set you free.

The experiential model: Get to the pain in your life, and then somehow "get it out."

The supernatural model: The Holy Spirit heals, sometimes instantly and sometimes gradually.

• What value do you see in each of the four models? (Pages 16 and 17 offer more details about each one.)

---

*The subtitles and page numbers refer to corresponding sections and pages in the book *How People Grow*.

- Which model makes the most sense to you and/or which model have you relied on—intentionally or otherwise—in your valleys? Why?

I connected most with the truth model, yet at the medical center I saw people who had walked with God for years and many who knew more about God's truth than I did. These people had been very diligent about prayer, Bible study, and other spiritual disciplines. Nevertheless, they were hurting, and for one reason or another, they had been unable to walk through their valley.

- When have you seen one of these models of personal growth fail a person—or when has one of these models failed you? What was the result, and why do you think the model failed?

The woman in the pink bathrobe was a missionary who had been called off the field because she was out of touch with reality. Other more normal clients had tried the things they knew to deal with marital, parenting, emotional, and work struggles, and they felt as though these spiritual answers had let them down. And I began to feel the same way. Again the realization hit me: *This is going to be harder than I thought.*

THE FAILURE OF THE TRUTH MODEL (Page 18)

People were getting better and gaining some relief through these four models. Prayer, learning Scripture, and repentance were very powerful elements in healing many clinical conditions. But something was missing. I did not see what I had gone into Christian counseling to see—namely, people's lives being transformed.

- When have you—or someone you know—hit an area of life that did not give way to your best spiritual efforts, whether prayer, Bible study, Christian service, or just "being good"? What was the area of life? What efforts to grow did you make?

- Currently, what area of your life does not seem to be changing despite your best spiritual efforts?

- What area of your life would you like to change?

I often saw high-functioning people who had followed Christian methods of growth as best they could but without success. I knew there had to be more.

BEING BORN AGAIN, AGAIN (Page 19)

I continued to work in Christian counseling, and something happened in the next four to five years that turned my world upside down. I saw people grow past their stuck places. I saw processes that actually changed people's lives; I found the "something more." But what helped people grow did not seem to be what I had been taught was the "Christian" way to grow.

- It seemed to me that there was the spiritual life, where we learned about God and grew in our relationship to him, and then there was the emotional and relational life, where we learned how to solve real-life problems. When have you sensed this disconnect between the life of God and your "real" life? Put differently, what areas of your life don't you expect "spiritual growth" to affect? Be specific.

But this disconnect made no sense. All of life is spiritual, and God is involved in every area of life. So how could there be spiritual growth and then "other" growth? I went back to the Bible to discover how spiritual growth addresses and solves life's problems—and I discovered that everything I had been learning that helped people grow was right there in the Bible all along. Not only was the Bible true, but what was true was in the Bible!

- Which of the following two emphases and/or three approaches are intriguing, encouraging, or exciting? (Review the discussion on pages 21 and 22.) Put differently, which make(s) you want to keep reading this book?

     We wanted people who came to us for counseling to understand that the issue(s) they were working on were not *growth* issues or *counseling* issues, but *spiritual growth* issues.

     We wanted to bring the idea of working on relational and emotional issues back into the mainstream of spiritual growth. Spiritual growth should affect relationship problems, emotional problems, and all other problems of life.

     We wanted those responsible for helping people grow to know *how* the spiritual and the practical are linked.

     We wanted those who were working with people to be aware of the things that deeply change people's lives.

     We wanted people who were growing to know not only how to grow, but that their growth was biblical growth.

For thirty years or so the church has become increasingly interested in personal growth, the resolution of relational or emotional problems, and their integration into church life. The spiritual and the practical have been addressed but not linked together with a biblical understanding.

ALL GROWTH IS SPIRITUAL GROWTH (Page 22)

In this book we would like, as best we can, to link the great doctrines of the Bible with how people grow spiritually, emotionally, and relationally. So three of the questions this book will answer are these: (1) What helps people grow? (2) How do these processes fit into our orthodox understanding of spiritual growth and theology? and (3) What are the responsibilities of the person helping others grow (pastor, counselor, group leader), and what are the responsibilities of the ones who are growing?

- Which of these questions interests you? Why?

- What other questions do you hope this book will answer? In other words, why are you reading this book?

Our desire is that the book be practical, that it help you understand how to help people grow. We also want it to be a book that enlightens you on how the growth process, at its very core, is theological.

BACK TO SEMINARY (Page 23)

As we offer a biblical perspective on how people grow, we will go through the major Christian doctrines and talk about how each doctrine applies to personal growth. Even though we won't always call them doctrines, you can rest assured that the major doctrines of the faith are the architecture of this book, as they are the architecture of all that we do. Here are the major doctrines and themes that we will apply to growth:

The theology of God	The Bible
The person of Christ	Poverty of spirit
The Holy Spirit	and brokenheartedness
The role of truth	Guilt and forgiveness
The role of grace	Confession
The role of sin and temptation	Discipline and correction
The created order	Obedience and repentance
The role of the Body of Christ	Suffering and grief
(the church)	The role of time

- Think about your own growth. Which of these items have contributed to your personal growth, not just your "spiritual" growth?

- Which of the items on the list surprise you? Why?

- What part of your life does this list invite you to think about differently? In other words, what aspect of your life or what life event might have been an opportunity for growth? What current aspect of your life or recent life event can you—with the help of this book and the resources it points you to—view as an opportunity for growth?

We're glad you're joining us as we take a look at what the Bible reveals about how people grow.

Lord God, it makes so much sense that we can't—and shouldn't try to—compartmentalize life into "spiritual life" and "real life" and, as a result, that spiritual growth is the answer to every problem I face. It's also exciting to realize that you, the author of life, are also the author of our growth. I look forward, Lord, to receiving from you the gift of growth as I work with the ideas in this book. I look forward to seeing what the Bible reveals about how people grow and to growing in ways that you would have me grow. I pray in Jesus' name. Amen.

TIPS FOR GROWERS:

- Consider the model of how people grow that you had before you opened the book. Note what specific changes in those preconceptions would give you a more biblical model.

- Identify any disconnect in your thinking between "real" life and spiritual life and growth. Note especially any areas you don't expect "spiritual growth" to affect.

CHAPTER TWO

Seeing the Big Picture

Many times, in the process of helping people grow, we forget the big picture of what God is doing in the human race. But the big picture—the story of God and his creation that was lost and of his work to restore or reconcile it to himself—is very important. As we enter into the specifics of people's lives, we must not lose sight of what God is doing in the world.

- The challenge faced by those who help people grow and by those who want to grow is this: to figure out ways that the Fall is operative in a person's life and discover a redemptive path that will "reconcile" his or her life. We are to be working with God as he reconciles all things "to himself" (2 Cor. 5:18–19). What benefits come with approaching a marriage problem, a parenting challenge, or depression from this perspective? After you complete this book, you'll be able to give a much more detailed answer, but jot down the thoughts you have now.

- Exactly what are we trying to reconcile? We are trying to get people back into relationship with God, with one another, and with the idea of holiness and pure living—but this is not enough. Spiritual growth is not only about coming back into a relationship with God and one another and about pursuing a pure life, but it is also about coming back to life—the life God created people to live. We must be reconciled to life the way it was created to work. However extensive or limited your knowledge of the Bible and of God's design for human beings, list what you know or glimpses you've had of what your life would look like if you lived God's way.

In the rest of this book, we will talk about how we believe this process works. But first let's look at the way God created life to begin with (Creation), what happened to that life (the Fall), and what God has said about getting it back (Redemption).

ACT ONE: CREATION (Page 28)

How was life designed to be lived? What is it supposed to look like?

Big Idea Number One: God Is the Source. Everything—the resources, the principles, the purposes, the meaning of life, as well as life itself—came from God. He is the Source, period.

- We understand that living things come from God. But we have to understand that God is also able to bring life to dead situations in our lives. God is not only the Creator but also the re-Creator of life.

  — Is "God is the Source" merely a belief you hold or a real practice in your life? How much time do you spend looking to God to hear how he can change your situation? How often do you look to him? Hourly? Daily? Weekly? Monthly?

  — Specifically, when have you seen God as the Source for resolving your life issues? What did you do to turn to him? What resulted from your looking to God as the Source?

  — What keeps you from looking to God as the Source of the resolution of current life issues?

  — Jesus tells us that an abiding, seeking, hungering, and knocking relationship is what makes God as Source available to us. What evidence is there in your life that you are abiding? What are you doing to seek and knock? How hungry are you to know God? What could you do to increase your hunger?

Many Christian systems of growth have many principles—even a lot of biblical principles—about God, but little or no God. Remember, God is the source of life. He is the source of growth as well.

Big Idea Number Two: Relationship. God put people into relationship, first with him and then with one another. God made people for himself and also for one another. And relationship was vulnerable and open, without duplicity and without brokenness or breach.

- Evaluate your relationship with God. What growth would you like to experience?

- What role do you see God playing in your relationship with him and with others?

- Where, if at all, are you experiencing the true vulnerability of Eden?

One aspect of genuine, healthy relatedness is that people don't hide their vulnerability from one another and are not ashamed of who they are before one another.

Big Idea Number Three: God Is the Boss. God created an order to our relationships. God was the Boss, the Lord, the Authority. He was in charge, and he gave us both positive and negative directions. We were to live life in submission to God, or we would not have life at all. Life and submission to God were one and the same. This is how things were supposed to be at Creation, but all of this changed and was lost.

- When have you seen life lived in rebellion to God bring death — spiritual, metaphorical, and/or even physical? Or when have you experienced this "death" for yourself? Describe the situation.

- When have you submitted to God and had a taste of life lived fully? Describe the experience.

- In what current circumstances are you choosing life? In what present situation are you choosing death? Explain each choice. Why did you make the choice? What have been the results?

The Bible begins with the ideas of God as Source, relationship as primary, and God as the authority — and the implications of this theology for how people grow are enormous.

Big Idea Number Four: Roles of God, Roles of People. God is the boss, and we are to obey. But there is more to this structure than just "who's on top." We are to have distinctly different roles in God's intended order of creation.

1. *God's role was to be the Source or Provider; our role was to depend on the Source.* The role we must take in life is not only *for* dependency, but also *against* self-sufficiency. Our role is to recognize our limits and to transcend those limits by looking outside of ourselves for life. We need God, and we need other people. We are limited in our ability to live alone, apart from God. And we cannot live independently from people either.

— What aspect of this truth is unsettling?

— What aspect is freeing?

— If you were taken to Eden's court, could you be convicted of being dependent in a good way? Cite specific evidence from your life.

The result of trying to live apart from our need for others is disastrous and never works. We must depend on the outside for love.

2. *God's role was to be in control; our role was to yield to God's control of the world and to control our self.* So many of people's problems come from trying to control things outside of their control, and when they try, they lose control of themselves.

— Think about problems you've had or a problem you're dealing with now. Was your attempt to control things outside of your control a factor that contributed to the problem? Explain.

— When have you seen a loss of self-control accompany a person's effort to control something beyond human control? Give an example, ideally from your own life.

God's role is to be in control of the big picture, and our role is to be in control of our self and our responsibilities—in short, to maintain "self-control."

3. *God was the Judge of Life; we were to experience life.* Another role that belonged to God was to know good from evil. He had that role from the beginning and did not want to pass it on to humanity. Likewise, we human beings were not to judge, but to live the good life apart from judging it. Instead of being concerned with "Am I good enough?" we were just to live and experience life.

— What do you appreciate about this perspective on God's command to Adam and Eve to stay away from the tree of knowledge of good and evil and to let him be God? What point was new to you?

— To what degree is the "Am I good enough?" question a concern for you? Let "1" mean "It never even crosses my mind" and "10" mean "I hardly think of anything else!"

— If your answer is closer to "1" than "10," to what do you attribute that freedom and what are you doing to preserve it? If your answer is closer to "10," when will you stop playing judge? Who will help you? Where will you go to find someone to help you, to pray for you, to hold you accountable?

We are to experience all that God has given us in pleasure, work, and relationship. God alone is judge, and in essence he says to us, "Don't assume that role."

4. *God made the rules; we were to obey them.* God designed life the way it was supposed to be and the rules for how to live it. We were to obey them.

— Which of God's rules have you ever wanted to rewrite? Give an example or two and explain how you wanted them revised.

— Which of God's rules are you currently disagreeing with? Why? In what ways is your disagreement manifesting itself in your life?

— When have you seen the wisdom and life-giving ability of God's rules, ideally one which you had earlier bucked or perhaps are bucking now? Be specific.

God made the reality and then told us to obey it.

The Whole Package. If you think about this picture, this is pretty much the life everyone is looking for: a great place to live, the perfect mate, lots of good things to occupy your time, and a job that fits your makeup.

• Which of these four elements in "the whole package" is causing you the greatest distress these days?

• What kind of struggle has resulted from your distress?

Instead of remaining the innocent crown of creation, we humans took a great tumble, which brings us to Act Two, where we try to gain independence, take control, become the judge, and make our own rules.

ACT TWO: THE FALL (Page 33)

What happened in the Fall to change how life was designed? What is the problem we are trying to fix?

• ***Reversing the Order:*** Adam and Eve decided that God's design was not for them. They believed the Tempter's implication that they would do well by rebelling against God and that they could be to themselves all that God was to have been to them. In the Fall, Adam and Even became separated from Life and missed the mark of all that life was created to be. They were in a strange state that the Bible calls "sin" or "death" (Eph. 2:1). They lost themselves, one another, and the life they were created to have.

1. *They became independent from the Source.* When Adam and Eve ate from the tree, they moved away from God and tried to gain life apart from him.

   — When have you seen someone move away from God and try to gain knowledge and wisdom apart from the Source? To what or whom did that person turn—and what were the consequences?

   — When have you tried to gain life outside of your relationship with God? Why did you make that effort, and what resulted?

   — Where are you seeking to gain life right now? Outside of your relationship with God? When will you turn—or turn back—to God?

Adam and Eve no longer needed God and had taken a step away from their role of dependency.

2. *They lost their relationships.* In addition to becoming independent from God, they lost their relationship with him as well as with one another. This is what death is. Their intimacy and vulnerability with one another was lost.

   — What taste of death, of separation from God, have you had or are you perhaps experiencing even now? Describe the circumstances.

   — What taste of death, of separation from human relationship, have you experienced or are you now experiencing? What were/are the consequences of that?

— Like Adam and Eve, what experiences of being emotionally "naked and ashamed" have you had in your relationships with people?

The relationship and intimacy Adam and Eve had with their Creator was lost; they had become separated from him. Also, love for one another became much harder to find and sustain.

3. *They reversed the structure and order.* In the creation, God was on top, and Adam and Eve answered to his authority. He was the lord, the ruler. But in the Fall, humans tried to usurp that structure and become their own lord.

— When have you, like Adam and Eve, rebelled against one of God's specific instructions? Be specific about your choice and its consequences.

— In what area(s) of your life are you currently attempting to be lord? Why?

Adam and Even tried to become "like God." They became self-sufficient and controlling. They were judgmental and lived by their own rules.

4. *They reversed the roles.* The chart below outlines the roles as God created them. In the Fall, humans tried to reverse this created order in their attempt to become like God.

God	Humans
God is the Source	We depend on God
God is the Creator	We are the creation and cannot exist unto ourselves
God has control of the world	We have control of ourselves
God was the judge of life	We are to experience life
God designed life and its rules	We obey the rules and live the life God designed

— We desired to control things we could not control, including one another, and we lost control of ourselves. Where do you see evidence of these two truths in the world around you and/or in your relationships?

— We tried to become the judge, and we ended up being judgmental instead. Where have you seen this point illustrated? When do you tend to be judgmental? Be specific on both counts.

— We stopped obeying God's design and rules and made up our own. What rules have you made up for yourself, or, perhaps easier to see, what rules has society made up for itself?

So life began with a particular plan, and this plan was usurped by rebellion against God, and life was lost. But God did not allow things to stay that way. He had another plan.

ACT THREE: REDEMPTION (Page 36)

The holy God required the death penalty for the sin of humankind, and he laid all of this sin on Jesus (Isa. 53:5–6). This paved the way for redemption, for God to return everything to its rightful order. God in Christ is "reconciling" all things, bringing them back to the way they are supposed to be. This is why, in our view, to solve life's problems and to grow spiritually are one and the same.

- **Return to the Source:** In redemption we come back to God as the source of life. We retreat from our independence from him and our attempt to be "self-made." Also, we find that God is the source of healing and growth, and we see that true growth begins with realizing that we are "poor in spirit." From this humble position, we reach out to God and receive all that he has for us (Matt. 5:3).

— Have you ever given up your attempt to be "self-made" and turned to God as the source of life? If so, when? What prompted that decision, and what have been the blessings of that choice?

— If you have not yet turned to the source of life and begun to experience the redemption and reconciliation that he offers you, what is keeping you? With whom can and will you discuss your concerns?

— When have you or someone you know experienced the truth that God is the source of healing and growth? Describe the situation.

Redemption helps us get to the end of our attempt to provide for ourselves. Recognizing our sin and, in a simple prayer, accepting Jesus' death on the cross as payment of the penalty for our sins is the way we turn to God, in whom we'll find strength, truth, healing, care, correction, and a whole host of other things. None of these things is available to those who are still trying to provide for themselves.

- ***Return to Relationship:*** To return to the created order means to get back into relationship with God and with one another. Everything in life depends on loving God and loving others (Matt. 22:37–40).

  — Redemption reconciles us to God, reestablishing a connection with him through our faith and his forgiveness. What are you doing to maintain a healthy connection with God? What would make your connection with God even stronger? When will you take that step—and who will pray for you and hold you accountable?

— Redemption also reconnects us with others as it stresses love, identification with one another through the Golden Rule, caring for one another, forgiving one another, healing one another, teaching one another, correcting one another, and so on. Which of these different kinds of connectedness with other believers is most threatening to you? Why? What will you do to overcome the obstacle(s) you just identified? Where will you go to find people with whom a safe connection is possible?

Redemption reverses our alienation and isolation from one another and gets us rightly reconnected.

- ***Return to the Order:*** Redemption is also a surrender to God as Lord. As Jesus said, the first and the greatest commandment is to love God. This commandment ensures that I am going to do life God's way, and if I do it his way, it will be better.

  — To reverse the Fall means to live under submission to God and to no longer rebel against his rulership in your life. What aspect of your life has been or continues to be a struggle to submit to God?

  — In what way could or does God's Holy Spirit help you in this struggle? In what ways could or does a body of fellow believers support you in your struggle? Be specific on both counts.

  — To disobey God is basically to ruin our life, for to disobey him means that we by definition are doing something destructive. Give an illustration of this principle from the world around you. In what area(s) of your life are you currently disobeying God and therefore doing something destructive that will ruin your life?

In redemption, we no longer have to destroy our life by doing things other than God's way. In spiritual growth, we stop doing the "deeds of death" and begin to do the things that lead to life.

- **Return to the Roles:** In the Fall we reversed the roles of humankind and God. We tried to fulfill his roles and then lost our ability to fulfill the ones we were created for. In redemption we reconcile things to the way they were supposed to be.

  — We become dependent on God and others. If you have ever done so, describe a time in your life when you gave up your independence. What resulted or is resulting? In what ways are you currently depending on God? On whom else are you depending?

  — We give up trying to control things we cannot control, and we yield to and trust God's control. We also regain the fruit of "self-control." What evidence of this have you seen in your life? If you aren't walking the path of redemption yet, what things beyond your control are you trying to control? What will it take for you to give up control?

  — We give up the role of playing judge with ourselves and others so that we are free to experience ourselves and others as we really are. What aspects of your personality have opened up since you or someone else stopped judging you? What people in your life do you see experiencing greater freedom to be themselves because you are no longer playing judge?

  — We stop redesigning life and making new rules and instead live the life God designed us to live. Give an example or two, past or present, of obeying God's laws and finding true freedom in doing so.

— Consider how you relate to God as Source, God as Boss, God as Judge, and God as Designer of life and Establisher of rules. In what area(s) do you struggle with your role (being dependent, obeying the rules, etc.)?

In redemption, we do life God's way.

WHAT DOES IT LOOK LIKE? (Page 40)

What God does in redemption and in our growth is so simple. At the same time, it is complicated and profound.

- What truth reviewed in Theology 101 (a.k.a. chapter 2) do you find especially challenging? Who will support you as you learn to live by it?

- What truth discussed here do you find especially hopeful? Again, who is supporting you as you live out that aspect of God's truth?

So how does the fall of humanity cause our problems, and how does the redemption process God set up cause us to grow and resolve life's issues? In the next chapter we will take a look at a real-life situation that illustrates this for us.

Lord God, the big picture is certainly an encouraging one! It's good to step back and realize that you are at work reconciling all things to yourself, that you are bringing things back to the way they are supposed to be. It's good to remember that you are not only the Creator of life but the re-Creator of life, that you are the source of growth, and that we find life when we submit to you. I want to do life your way, Lord. Teach me, I pray. In Jesus' name. Amen.

TIPS FOR GROWERS:

- Look at your life and life issues from the perspective of the Bible's account of what God is doing in the world.

- Explain why it is important for you to understand the whole of the Bible and God's sovereign plan for history.

- Determine how the specific issues discussed in this chapter relate to you.
  — God as Source
  — Relationship
  — God Is the Boss
  — Roles of God, Roles of People

CHAPTER THREE

How the Big Picture Affects the Small

Rich and Stephanie had both tried to make their life together work. When I met them, this couple, who had led many others through discipleship and spiritual growth, were unable to make it work for themselves, and I could tell it was from no lack of effort. They had diligently walked paths of spiritual growth for twenty-five years. It broke my heart to see two people so committed to God feel as if his ways of living hadn't influenced their lives more deeply than they had. They had followed him and ended up in a miserable place.

The good news is that Rich and Stephanie are now living the marriage they had always wanted. Their story reveals how healing occurs when we do what we talked about in the previous chapter: reconcile life to the way God created it, to the created order. It also gives us some insight into how people can be involved in "spiritual growth" for years without significant areas of their life changing.

A RETURN TO THE CREATED ORDER (Page 44)

When I first met Rich and Stephanie, they modeled all the things we talked about in the previous chapter under Act Two. The Fall reigned in their lives: They were not being "reconciled" to the way things were supposed to be. Much biblical growth was missing. To understand what makes reconciliation effective, let's look specifically at what was missing in their lives.

- *God as Source:* Without realizing it, Rich and Stephanie had turned away from depending on God as the source of everything they needed and toward depending on themselves. Subtly, the Spirit was slowly shut out.

— In what areas of your life are you similar to Rich and his way of slowly shutting out the Holy Spirit? How often, for instance, do you pray to God for the whole of your work, but not for the little day-to-day things you struggle with?

— What action step does this discussion of God as Source encourage you to take? When will you take that step? Who will pray for you and hold you accountable?

- **Relationship as Primary:** Rich and Stephanie were connected to a lot of people, but their relationships were not changing them or helping them grow up. They did not see friendships with others as a God-given source of growth and healing.

  — Love from other members of Christ's Body could have helped heal Rich of his insecurities and Stephanie of her fears of not being in control, issues that led to much of the quarreling in their marriage. Which of your hurts, past or present, can love from the Body of Christ help heal?

  — What keeps you from being involved in a healing community and/or from receiving all of God's grace that he would give you through them? What will you do to overcome the roadblock(s) you identified?

- **God as Boss:** Rich and Stephanie were committed to God as Lord of their lives, but they submitted very little to God in their day-to-day internal lives. In the midst of their disconnection, in their attitudes toward each another, or in the way they handled their own stress, they pretty much answered to themselves. It was, however, their submission to "God as Boss" that saved their marriage.

— To what current situation in your life does the fact that God is boss speak? In other words, in what situation are you not letting him be boss—and what difference might letting him take that rightful role make?

— What action step does this discussion of God as boss encourage or even convict you to take? When will you take that step? Who will pray for you and hold you accountable?

Rich and Stephanie allowed God to be boss in their lives, and they obeyed him. As a result, their marriage was saved. God as Boss ultimately made everything else possible.

RESTORING THE ROLES (Page 48)

- *God as Source, People as Dependent:* We were created finite, not self-sustaining. Therefore we have to look outside of ourselves to get the things we need. This includes depending on God for everything and depending on others for what we cannot give ourselves.

  — What unfinished parts of you need healing and growth?

  — For what are you not depending on God? What aspect(s) of your life are you not sharing with him?

  — What keeps you from depending on people? What will you do to get past those obstacles?

— With whom are you able to share your deepest fears, hurts, and temptations? If the list of people is short, where might you go to find such relationships?

The Body of Christ is a big part of the delivery system of healing and growth that God has in store for people. For the Body to truly function in a healing way, we all have to reclaim dependency as well as serve. We were created to be dependent, on God and on one another.

- ***God in Control, People Yielding to His Control and Developing Self-Control:*** Both Rich and Stephanie needed to trust God to control what happened in their lives and in their marriage. Self-control was the fruit of giving up the God role and regaining the human role of yielding.

  — Coming from a chaotic background, Stephanie tried hard to control Rich. Similarly, Rich tried to control what Stephanie thought of him, because he could not stand for her to think negatively of him. How are you trying to control something or someone? Explain.

  — Stephanie needed to learn to trust God to be in control of her life, and Rich needed to learn to give God control of what happened in their lives and their marriage. Think again about the controlling behavior you just described. What do you need to trust God to control? Put differently, what do you need to leave in God's hands?

  — When have you seen or perhaps experienced for yourself the regaining of self-control that comes with relinquishing attempts to control circumstances or other people? Why do you think this happens?

The growing freedom both Rich and Stephanie gained by giving up external control and regaining internal control revolutionized their relationship.

- ***God as Judge of Life and People as Experiencers of Life:*** A key component of growth is grace—enough grace to open up and bring things into the light to be healed. Judgment, however, keeps us from bringing all of who we are into relationship to be healed and to grow.

  — What point about the difference between "judging not" and confronting one another's sin was new and/or especially helpful?

  — Under whose judgment do you feel you sit? What fears or needs might lie behind that person's behavior?

  — Whose judge have you appointed yourself to be? What fears or needs are behind your behavior? What might be a better way to express those fears or meet those needs?

  — To whom can you apologize for trying to play judge in his or her life? When will you do so?

A person getting out from under the control of another is powerfully free. This freedom leads to autonomous functioning and self-control, an essential ingredient of responsibility.

- ***God as Rule Maker, People as Rule Keepers:*** Rich and Stephanie did not see their violation of God's principles as the way into the mess they were in, nor did they see obeying his principles as the way out. Like ours, their doubts about God's rules were much more subtle and unconscious than Adam and Eve's, but their doubts were deadly nevertheless.

— When life is not working (and Rich and Stephanie's marriage was not working), it often means that some of God's ways are being violated, either willfully by us or by sin done to us. Consider an aspect of your life that is not working right now. Which of God's ways are being violated? By whom?

— To get well, Rich and Stephanie had to rediscover the idea that God's design and ways were given to make life work. Rich had to regain his ownership of the power of powerlessness and weakness, and Stephanie had to discover again that judgment belongs to God alone. Which of God's principles do you need to align yourself with to find healing and wholeness? Cite a specific biblical teaching if you can. Define the first step you will take in your alignment or realignment with God's principles—and plan when you will take it.

Not many serious Christians overtly say to God that his ways are not to be taken seriously. But when we live more according to our own design than God's, we suffer.

MOVING PAST THE BEGINNING (Page 59)

To make life work and to help others grow toward a life that works, we must remember two things.

• First, there are foundational principles without which nothing else works. If we do not live according to the foundations of the faith, we will have nothing secure to build upon.

— List what you think some of these "foundational principles" are. (God's foundation will be described more completely in the rest of the book.)

— Why does the Christian faith offer the only secure foundation for your life?

- Second, the foundational things are not all there is to growth. There is a process that takes us from the "foundation" to "maturity," or completeness. We must learn more than the elementary principles of the faith.

   — Have you, like Rich and Stephanie, learned the elementary principles of the faith and, over time, forgotten them? Or have you tried to make the elementary things the entire picture of spiritual growth? Support your answer with specific details from your life.

   — At this point, what do you think the process of growth from "foundation" to "maturity" might involve for you?

In the following chapters, we will show both God's foundation and how to use it and also "go on to maturity" by looking at the rest of the story beyond the foundation. Join us now as we begin that journey.

Lord God, it is far too easy for me to be lord of my life, to not even consult you in the moment-by-moment decisions of my day. And in the busyness of life, I not only shut you out, but I shut out people as well. I don't make relationship primary. Forgive me, Lord, and teach me, I pray, to be dependent on you and on your people, to yield to your control and to develop self-control, to stop judging others, and to keep your rules and live according to your design. And please empower me with your Holy Spirit, because I know I can't do these things on my own. I pray in Jesus' name. Amen.

TIPS FOR GROWERS:

- Note at what points your own life connects with Rich and Stephanie's story.
- Cite any evidence from your life that . . .
  — you realize God is the Source of returning you to life

  — real relationship with God is primary in your life instead of merely religious duty

  — real relationship with others is primary instead of just a principle to which you give lip service

  — community and relationship is the delivery system for what God provides for you

  — God is the boss or master of your life. Also identify the cracks in your submission to him as Lord
- Evaluate how well you are playing the following human roles. Support your answer with specific evidence from your life.
  — Being dependent
  — Having self-control and not being controlling of others and life
  — Experiencing life and others instead of judging yourself and others
  — Obeying the rules instead of writing them

PART TWO

The Master Gardener: The God of Growth

CHAPTER FOUR

The God of Grace

The answers to life and all of its issues are found in seeking God and his righteousness. He really is there, and he really is the answer. So in this chapter we will look at how a relationship with God "grows life." We will look at concepts that might seem elementary to some—but ones of which we need to be continually reminded—and at how those concepts help us grow. If they are present, we believe that growth cannot help but occur.

A TRUE VIEW OF GOD (Page 66)

One of the biggest obstacles to growth is our view of God. If we are going to grow in relation to God, then we must know who God is and what he is really like. People do not grow until they shift from a natural human view of God to a real, biblical view of God.

- The first aspect of that shift has to be the shift from a God of law to the God of grace. People must discover that God is *for* them and not *against* them.

   —Define *grace*, mentioning what it is not as well as what it is. Feel free to quote from the book.

   —When we are under the law—in our natural state—we feel that God was the enemy and that we get what we deserve. We naturally try to "earn" life. We try to save ourselves. When have you felt that God was your enemy? How have you tried to earn his approval, to earn life? What are you doing now? Be specific.

— Look again at Dirk, his life under the law, and the glimpse into what his life might be like if he lived under grace (pages 68–69). What does Dirk's life under grace suggest to you about what your life would look like if you lived under grace? Again, be specific.

— What problem in your life are you trying to fix by your own efforts?

— In what areas of your life are you guilty of seeing grace as merely forgiveness or the absence of condemnation? What does it mean in each of those contexts that God is *for* you?

A view of God that affects growth must begin with grace. This "grace" is God's provision of various resources and tools to help us grow. We do not grow because of "willpower" or "self-effort," but because of God's provision. God offers the help we need (that's grace), and then we have to respond to that provision.

PRACTICAL THEOLOGY (Page 69)

Understanding grace is not just a theological exercise; it is essential to constructing a system of growth.

• When have you bumped up against this common evangelical mode for change: being asked if you are living up to the standard, being forgiven if you are not, and then being encouraged to go out and do better? Or are you holding on to this model for others to bump up against?

- When have you been received as a person "standing in grace" and not condemned, even in failure? Or when have you known that you were unable to stop a behavior just by trying harder and you were directed to places where you could be given what you could not provide for yourself (support, structure, healing, and help with the appetites driving the behavior)? Or when have you been involved in helping a person experience this kind of "standing in grace"?

- Where will you go — and when — to be received as a person "standing in grace," even in failure? Or where will you go — and when — to find support, structure, healing, and help for a behavior you are unable to stop just by trying harder? And to whom will you give the opportunity to experience this kind of "standing in grace"?

- What does it mean to you that, in Christ, there is "no condemnation" (Rom. 8:1)? What does it mean to have a "standing in grace" (see Romans 5:1)? Which of your thoughts and behaviors suggest that you know God not as an enemy but as one who wants to help you? Be specific.

- When have you experienced failure and then chosen to avoid God, thinking he was mad at you, rather than turn to him? When have you experienced failure and then chosen to run to God and the people you needed? What motivated each choice? What resulted from each choice?

- Are you currently choosing to avoid God rather than turning to him? If so, why? Or are you running to God and the people you need? If not, why not—and when will you run to God? And where will you go to find safe, accepting people?

- Finally, when have you experienced the kind of unmerited favor we suggested earlier for Dirk? What resources did people provide you?

For growth to happen, first, emphasis on the law must be eliminated. The law will make things worse, not better (Rom. 5:20; 7:10). Second, we must recognize our need for grace.

GETTING TO THE NEED FOR GRACE (Page 71)

Grace is only effective when there is a need for it. The law is powerless to change people or make them grow (Rom. 8:3), but it does provide awareness of "spiritual death," which people need to find the God who seeks them.

- The law makes us conscious of our need for God (Rom. 3:20; Gal. 3:24) and shows us that we can't help ourselves. Describe how this truth worked itself out in your life.

- In growth as well as in salvation, people must experience a need to get to a place of grace. They must be aware of death. I (Henry) experienced the death of all my dreams and of my ability to find a life that worked. When have you also gotten to the end of yourself and become a candidate for grace? Did you receive God's grace? Why or why not? Or are you a candidate for grace right now? What is keeping you from receiving God's grace? What will you do to overcome that interference?

- Rich and Stephanie needed to realize that their love had died and that they were powerless to revive that love. When they realized that, they were ready for God's grace. They were ready to turn to him and receive the things he had to offer. What current situation is helping you recognize your powerlessness? What is keeping you from turning to God for his grace?

We sometimes need a funeral director to show us that we have to die not only to the law, but also to ourselves. That funeral director can help us recognize that all of our efforts have not worked and that we need to die to trying. And sometimes we need to be such a funeral director and allow someone else to come to these realizations.

HELPING OTHERS GET TO THE NEED FOR GRACE
(Page 72)

- **Confrontation:** Confrontation is an important tool to get someone to see both his inability to change and his need for help.
  — Law is a way to help a person know his need or to show a person that she is not living up to a standard. How has someone used the law to help you see your need for help? How have you used the law to help someone else see his or her inability to change? Be specific about both confrontations.

  — What aspect of the account of the woman who hadn't had a date in three years was helpful to you? How did this real-life scenario help you appreciate confrontation?

People will never get to the end of themselves if they do not see themselves as failing. Confrontation can help speed this realization about themselves.

- *Reality Consequences and Discipline:* Allowing people to suffer logical consequences is another way of getting them to realize their need for grace. When people cannot (or do not) hear the truth of confrontation, we often have to allow reality to touch their lives.

  — When has someone helped you by letting you experience the tough realities that ultimately led you to the grace you needed? Be specific about the tough realities as well as the grace you experienced once you were open to receiving it.

  — What tough realities are you currently experiencing? What grace is available to you?

  — When have you let someone hit bottom—lose a job, a relationship, and so on— so that she could see her need for God and what he has to offer her? What truths enabled you to stand strong? What was the person's reaction to you and your actions both immediately and later on? What was the long-term result of this person hitting bottom?

  — Is there someone in your life whom you could let hit bottom so that she can see her need for God? Why are you hesitating to let her?

  — What lesson from the story of the prodigal son strengthens the argument for reality consequences?

Consequences that lead to grace are an act of grace in themselves (Heb. 12:4–11; James 1:2–4). So, in thinking about growth, leave room for people to fail. Reality consequences are not all bad. They are part of God's plan.

- ***Putting Grace and Truth Together:*** In summary, we have seen how a relationship with God affects growth.

   — First, to have growth that makes life work, we have to seek God. What are you doing or could you be doing to seek God?

   — Second, we need to realize that God is the God of grace and that grace is more than forgiveness. Grace means that we receive the gifts we need for growth to occur. What gifts—what grace—have you seen God bestow on someone so that that person could grow? What gifts has God given you—or are you aware of him giving you now—so that you could grow? Be specific.

   — Third, grace does not come easily, and we do not naturally recognize it. It only comes in the classroom of God's law. When have you seen someone admit her failure to attain God's standard and thereby die to self? Or when have you seen someone experience the consequences of having life fall short of God's standards and thus come to the end of himself? What role did God's law play in your dying to yourself?

   — What failure to attain God's standard do you need to confess? When will you do that—and to whom?

— What gifts of grace are you in need of right now for the truth of a current life situation to change? Where will you get those gifts? "I don't know" cannot be your final answer. The God of grace *will* provide. Keep seeking. What are some other places you can look? Who can help you?

We must realize that we have failed and that we have no hope of reaching the life we desire in and of ourselves. After that, the law of God guides us, empowered by grace, to structure life as it was created to be. His principles are a "lamp unto our feet."

Lord God, thank you for failure in my life, thank you for helplessness, thank you for your standards, which are impossible for me to live up to, and thank you for the consequences of my sinful actions. Oh, some of these things have brought great pain, but you have used them—or you can use them—to help me see my need for you. Help me to continue to die to myself, moment by moment, so that—like your Son—I may do your will, not mine; that I may be both a recipient and channel of your grace. I pray in Jesus' name. Amen.

TIPS FOR GROWERS:

- Explain when and/or why you see God as *for* you, *against* you, or perhaps both.

- Identify from whom and/or in what situations you are receiving grace. If you aren't receiving such "unmerited favor," determine where you will go to get it.

- To get to a place of grace, you must experience a need. List any current needs and prayerfully consider your openness to receiving God's grace in each situation.

- Describe any reality consequences with which you are already dealing.

CHAPTER FIVE

Jesus: Our Example for Living

Jesus plays a unique role in the spiritual growth process. I (John) cannot imagine genuine spiritual maturity without the contributions of Jesus. So, in this chapter, we will look at several specific areas in which Jesus helps people grow.

THE ONGOING RELATIONSHIP (Page 80)

First, Jesus is "with" us (Matt. 28:20). Jesus has gone to be with the Father, but he also lives in the heart of each believer (1 Cor. 3:16). By faith and in some mysterious way, he lives inside us (Eph. 3:17). This means we have an ongoing, sustaining relationship with Jesus.

- People need two sorts of relationships to grow: the divine and the human. Describe your connection to the indwelling Christ. In what situations do you turn to him? When are you most aware of him? For what aspects of your life are you most dependent on him? For what aspects of your life are you choosing independence? Why?

- Connection to the indwelling Christ involves learning to become aware of Jesus. What can you do to become more aware of, responsive to, and dependent on Jesus minute by minute? When will you start?

- Do you have trouble trusting God? Are you self-sufficient and insular? Do you regard relationships, including a relationship with Jesus, as dangerous? If so, what has contributed to this distrust and independence? What steps will you take to gain or regain the ability to be in a relationship and trust someone? See our books *Changes That Heal* and *Hiding from Love* for some ideas.

With Jesus we have a personal, living connection with God. This is a tremendous source of good things—things like good fruit (John 15:5), answers to prayer (John 15:7), power (2 Cor. 12:9), and peace (Col. 3:15)—which people need for spiritual growth.

IDENTIFICATION (Page 81)

Another way Jesus is essential to spiritual growth is called identification. He serves as a model who can teach and comfort us in many growth situations. Biblical principles tell us how people grow; Jesus shows us. In Jesus, we have a living, breathing picture of how God wants us to live.

- What does Jesus show us about the biblical principle of submitting to God's will? See, for instance, Matthew 26:36–46.

- In what current situation can you follow Jesus' model and submit to God's will?

- What does Jesus show us about the biblical principle of doing for others what you would have them do for you?

- In what current situation can you follow Jesus' model and do for others what you would have them do for you?

The bulk of this chapter will show those aspects of identification with Jesus that apply to people's growth.

RESPONSE TO SUFFERING (Page 82)

One of the most important tasks of spiritual growth is to understand how to suffer. Although suffering is negative, it is part of life. No one grows to maturity who does not understand suffering.

- ***Normalize Suffering:*** Jesus taught that we would have trials and tribulations in this world (John 16:33), and he shows us much about how to respond to suffering. Most important is that he did not avoid suffering but saw it as part of the growth path (Heb. 5:8).

  — When have you seen someone grow as a result of pain and suffering—or when have you noticed growth in yourself? Note briefly the suffering and describe the growth.

  — What current situations in your life could be the source of growth? Remember that those circumstances are not beyond God's control, but that he uses them to grow you into the person he wants you to be.

- ***Choose Godly Suffering:*** Jesus is a wonderful example of embracing needful suffering and rejecting that which was not. He understood that pain must have a purpose. He chose the path of the Cross because of the fruit it would bear for all of us. Yet he refused to enter suffering inappropriate to his purposes and not in line with God's timetable for his death (John 10:39).

— When have you not avoided some suffering that you would have been wise to avoid? Or when have you seen someone else in such a situation? What kept you or that person in that place of suffering?

— If you're suffering now and you realize that you would have been wise to avoid such suffering, why are you still there? What is keeping you in that place of suffering?

— When have you avoided what could have been good pain? Or when have you seen someone do this? Why did you or that person choose the path of avoidance?

— What good pain are you avoiding now? Why?

- **Be Humble:** One way to bear necessary pain is to be humble. Being humble means not perceiving ourselves to have rights or privileges that we do not possess. We certainly do not have to pretend to enjoy the pain, and we should allow others to comfort us in it. But humility is a necessary trait for bearing pain. Jesus is a wonderful example of the value of humility in suffering rightly: He humbled himself and underwent pain he didn't bring on himself (Phil. 2:6–7).

  — The opposite of humility is grandiosity, a defense mechanism that prevents us from suffering rightly. Some people deny the experience, others insist their righteousness should prevent their suffering, and still others attempt to avoid suffering altogether. Give an example of when you or someone you know has chosen one of these paths when suffering came his or her way. What growth might have come had you or that person chosen the path of humility?

— In what present situation are you denying the experience, insisting that your righteousness should have prevented your suffering, or trying to avoid suffering altogether? What would be a better path? What first step on that path will you take—and when will you take it?

— When have you or someone you know (or know about) chosen the path of humility through painful times? Describe the circumstances and share your thoughts on why being humble was a wise and even beneficial approach.

— In what present and painful situation are you choosing—or could you be choosing—the path of humility? What are the benefits of your choice?

- **Depend on God and People:** We can't bear life on our own, nor were we created to do so. Jesus did not model independence, but dependence. Jesus was dependent on God and people (Matt. 6:11; 26:38).

   — What evidence of your dependence on God do you see when you look back on the past seven days? The past twenty-four hours? What do your answers tell you about yourself?

   — What evidence of your dependence on people do you see when you look back on the past seven days? The past twenty-four hours? What do these answers reveal to you about yourself?

— Think back to a time of suffering in your life. In what ways did you depend on God? On people? What difference did that dependence make—or what difference could it have made had you chosen it?

— In what current set of circumstances could you be choosing to depend more on God and people? When will you start depending on God? What step of depending on people will you take—and when?

Even though we are "in Christ" and we know that everything will ultimately be okay, here on earth today things aren't yet okay. We have much work to do before we celebrate the final victory, and some of that work involves normalizing suffering, choosing godly suffering, being humble, and depending on God and people.

RESPONSE TO BEING SINNED AGAINST (Page 84)

A specific type of suffering we must endure is suffering caused by being sinned against. We bring a great deal of pain to our lives by our own transgressions (sins by us); at the same time, others inflict much injury on us (sins against us). Jesus provides us a way to look at injury that helps us grow closer to God and also grow in character. Here are some tools for dealing with suffering caused by others.

1. *Acknowledge the wound, don't deny it.* When we are hurt emotionally, we tend to deny it. Just saying or pretending that something doesn't hurt us doesn't make it go away, and the wounded heart stays injured.

   — Is denying hurt a reflex action for you? Think back on a recent injury. Did you acknowledge—or are you acknowledging—the pain? Why or why not?

   — Jesus didn't pretend everything was okay when it wasn't. What past or present hurts can you look at again, this time being more open about the reality of the pain to give your wounded heart a chance to heal?

2. *Stay connected, don't isolate.* We tend to withdraw from relationship when we are hurt. Some people are afraid of their dependencies on others. Others feel guilty about burdening friends with their problems. Still others try to be self-sufficient. None of these responses helps a person heal and grow.

— Why do you tend to withdraw from relationship when you are hurt? What benefits might you have received from staying connected to God and/or people?

— What current pain or life challenge presents you with the choice to stay connected or to isolate yourself from people? What are you choosing and why?

— Jesus' way is not the way of detachment, but of emotional dependency on God and others. What do you want to do the next time you're hurting? What relationships will you rely on?

3. *Love and forgive, don't retaliate.* People also "naturally" lash back when they are hurt, and they desire revenge on the one who hurt them. It is a work of God in someone's life to not retaliate against one who has wounded him or her. Furthermore, retaliation is more likely to help the person who hurt you justify his own bad behavior even more.

— When have you been tempted to retaliate (or perhaps even tried it)? What kept you from retaliating (or what resulted from your attempt to retaliate)? Why would love and forgiveness have been a better course of action?

— Jesus calls us not to "exact" revenge, but he isn't saying we should never protect ourselves from hurt. We need to look at each situation individually and work out how much to protect ourselves without vengeance. What recent or current situation is an opportunity for you (or someone you know) to protect yourself without vengeance? To whom can you be offering love and forgiveness? Describe what that might look like. What will you do to start offering that person love and forgiveness—and when will you start?

4. *Practice self-control, don't be controlled.* Our initial response to being hurt is that we lose self-control. And many times we transfer power to the person who has hurt us.

— Remember the man who realized that his parents had been emotionally unresponsive to him all his life (page 87)? When have you seen someone be controlled by a person who hurt him or her by making that person the focus of thoughts, emotions, and even actions—or when have you let yourself be controlled by someone who hurt you? More specifically, in what relationship have you lost self-control to someone because you are in denial about how much that person hurt you and your denial keeps you from working through the pain and getting free of it?

— When people hurt Jesus, he did not allow it to change his values or direction in life. This trait is called self-control. People who are hurt need to confess and process pain, but they may also need to take back ownership of their lives. What person who has hurt you still has some control over you? Describe that control and consider what you might do to break its hold on you.

We do not always respond righteously or wisely to stresses and hurts in our lives. Such unrighteous and unwise responses come easily to us, but they do not help us grow. The path of growth is based on the example Jesus gave us: acknowledge the wound, stay connected to God and people, love and forgive, and practice self-control.

AUTHORITY OVER EVIL (Page 87)

Our own evil tendencies, those of others, and the influence of the Devil himself can be major stumbling blocks to the growth process. We can, however, identify with Jesus in his authority over evil. God has placed all things under Jesus' feet (Eph. 1:22), and that includes authority over sin and evil. We can take the delegated authority Jesus gives over evil (Matt. 10:1) and apply it to our own lives.

- *Zero Tolerance:* Jesus did not deny evil's existence. He knew about sin. Yet he did not approve of sin; he acted against it.

  — A man didn't see his drinking as a problem. He thought his problem was a controlling and perfectionistic wife. What sin in your life have you grown to be quite comfortable with, rationalizing it or seeing it as someone else's problem?

  — What will you do to take a zero-tolerance stance toward that sin you just identified? Who will hold you accountable?

- *Spiritual Warfare:* Evil exists in the form of a personal Devil. Jesus has overcome Satan's power by his death, and he has destroyed the Devil's work (1 John 3:8). Yet the Devil continues his attacks against people for now. Truly a spiritual battle is going on (Eph. 6:12).

  — When have you been aware of the spiritual battle in your own life? What did you do to stand strong—or what will you do when you sense the Devil attacking?

  — The Devil is certainly behind any injury designed to separate people from God, others, and growth. But psychological issues and possible medical causes are also important matters to consider when determining the roots of a problem. Don't look for a demon behind every problem—but also don't forget to consider that possibility. Which tendency do you have: to blame everything on the Devil or forget that his power is very real? What will you do to gain a more balanced approach to life's problems?

Jesus' zero-tolerance stance toward sin and his own confrontation with the Devil (Matt. 4:1–11) are two aspects of his authority that we can apply to our own lives.

DEALING WITH TEMPTATION (Page 89)

Many temptations lie along the path of growth. Jesus' stance toward temptation is instructive, especially as revealed in his own temptation (Matt. 4:1–11).

- People who want more of God and want to mature in their character often find that their temptations don't decrease, but the temptations change according to what they are working on. When have you seen this pattern in your own life? Describe the temptations and how they corresponded to the issue(s) you were working on. Why should this pattern not surprise us?

- Satan tempted Jesus to get his needs met in ways other than God's; to control God rather than to trust him and his ways; and to avoid suffering. Review Matthew 4:1–11. What did Jesus do in response to these temptations? What are you doing to stand strong against the Devil?

When we follow Jesus' path, we may suffer, but that suffering is a very small price to pay for the spiritual growth that results.

JESUS' IDENTIFICATION WITH OUR SUFFERING (Page 90)

There is another type of identification that deeply assists our growth: Jesus' ability to say about our situation, "I've been there." When we suffer, Jesus both assists us (Heb. 2:18) and feels compassion for us (4:15).

- **Completing the Role of High Priest:** As the one who is our advocate and representative before a righteous God, he had to be able to identify with those he represented. Jesus knows our suffering at a very personal level. Experience is the only gate through which he could have gained that knowledge of us, and he did it at a terrible cost.

  — When have you been able to offer another person your heartfelt compassion because of your own experience with suffering or with temptation to sin? Or when has someone else's experience with suffering made him or her able to offer you genuine compassion? Describe why this kind of connection was meaningful.

  — What does it mean to you that Jesus feels your frailties with you? To what current situation does this truth speak?

- **Receiving Empathy:** One of the most important aspects to growth in our suffering is that we need to know we are understood. This is what Jesus' identification provides. When we realize that he "gets it" because of his suffering, we are buoyed up and can continue down the path.

  — When have you especially sensed another person's genuine compassion for what you were going through? Be specific, especially about how helpful it was and perhaps why it was helpful.

  — When have you resisted empathy that was available to you from God and other people—or are you doing so now? What did you do—or are you doing—to hide from the empathy available to you from God and others?

— Where are you going to find empathy for life's current challenges and hurts?

— When have you felt compassion for someone who was suffering? What experience of suffering from your life enabled you to be empathic?

• ***Confronting Distance from God:*** Another benefit of Jesus' identification with us is that it leaves us without excuse when we want to turn from God in our pain. If we can say that no one truly understands our life, it helps us feel justified to stay out of the growth path.

— We have a natural tendency to think that no one understands the uniqueness of our particular situation. Why do you think that is?

— Why do you think the Devil often fans into full flame our doubts that someone could understand our pain?

— Since you do not have the excuse that God does not understand your situation, what do you have to do now?

God the Father and Jesus the Son both powerfully guide how people grow. In the next chapter, find out how the Holy Spirit is just as important in the process.

Lord Jesus, that you live in the heart of believers is a mystery I don't understand. I want to live more in the reality of your ongoing, sustaining relationship with me. I want to learn to become more aware of you and dependent on you. Please teach me to do so. I also ask that I would learn to follow your example in many areas—that I would normalize suffering, choose godly suffering, be humble, and depend more fully on God and other people. And when I'm sinned against, please help me to—as you did—acknowledge the wound, stay connected to God and people, love and forgive, and practice self-control. I know I can't do any of this without the power of your indwelling Spirit or the grace of your character. So I ask in faith, trusting that this spiritual growth is your will for me. Amen.

TIPS FOR GROWERS:

- Examine your assumptions about the role Jesus plays in your growth. Look at any tendencies to see him only in his Savior role and not involved in your life today.

- Explore the suffering Jesus experienced. Note at what points you can identify with his suffering as well as what points of your suffering he understands. In addition, look at the attitude toward suffering he models for you.

- Develop an awareness of how to make suffering normal, be humble when experiencing it, and not retaliate when you are hurt.

CHAPTER SIX

The Holy Spirit

For reasons we do not fully understand, Jesus decided to go to heaven and work on us from there, and he sent the Holy Spirit to be with us and produce the growth and change we seek. He said that this is better than his being here himself. Therefore, it must be incredible to have the Holy Spirit in our lives. Let's take a look at the ways he furthers our growth process.

THE INITIATOR AND THE COMPLETER (Page 95)

The Spirit begins the process of growth by wooing us to Jesus, and he is working to finish the task.

- Look back on how the Holy Spirit wooed (or is wooing) you to Jesus. What evidence of God's gracious plan do you see in your life?

- Philippians 1:6 offers great hope and encouragement. What particular aspect of your life or your growth process does this truth speak to right now?

We can trust the growth process, no matter how we feel in the midst of it. The Holy Spirit is always going to be there, drawing us to God and to greater and greater growth.

- **Security:** To grow and change we have to first know we are secure. The Holy Spirit gives us this security about our relationship with God (Eph. 1:13; 4:30).

    — Do you know you are secure in your relationship with God? Why or why not?

    — What do you believe about who Jesus is and why he died on the cross?

If you believe that Jesus is the Christ and you trust him for the forgiveness of your sins, that is proof you are sealed with the Holy Spirit (1 John 4:2; 5:10). You can stop worrying about whether your relationship with God is secure and get on with the work of growth.

- **The Partnership:** Beyond the security and assurance the Spirit provides, what does the work of the Spirit look like day to day? What does he do? The Holy Spirit comes alongside us and helps us in a variety of ways, some of which are listed below (supporting Scripture references are given in the text, pages 97–98).

    The Holy Spirit never leaves us.

    He will search our hearts and show us what we need to change.

    He will give us the abilities to do things we need to do, even gifts for work, or wisdom, or words to say when we don't know what to say.

    He will lead us and guide us.

    He will show us truth and teach us.

    He will counsel us and help us.

    He will help us live the life we need.

    He will fill us and control us.

    He will correct us and convict us.

    He will change us.

    He will give us gifts to help one another and put the Body of Christ together.

    — Which of these works of the Holy Spirit have you experienced in your life? Give a specific example of two or three items on the list.

— Which aspects of the Holy Spirit's work would you especially like to experience now? Be specific as you pray and ask him to act in your life.

God promises that all these gifts of the Holy Spirit are available to us. The problem becomes the "how." *How* does the Holy Spirit do it? How can we get him to do it?

- **A Mystery:** We cannot reduce the work of the Holy Spirit to a formula. The Holy Spirit cannot be controlled. But we can do what the Bible tells us to do: Ask for him to be in our lives and to help us. God promises us that if we ask for the Spirit, he will come (Luke 11:9–13).

  — If there is a formula to how the Spirit works in our lives, it is to seek him, ask for him, and then follow him. What aspect of this discussion of the Holy Spirit (more complete on pages 98–99 of the text) is new to you and/or most exciting?

  — The best way to think about the Holy Spirit and growth is to think about a moment-by-moment relationship of dependency on him. We depend on him to guide us, lead us, talk to us, reveal truth to us, empower us to do what we can't do, and many other things. But all this happens in an "abiding" way. We yield to him and follow. We give ourselves to him as we live out the life of growth. What action step will you take as a result of these truths about how the Holy Spirit partners with us for growth? Hint: Prayer is action!

The old way of trying to "do it right" by ourselves is over (Gal. 2:16, 19). Now we live a life of faith with the Holy Spirit inside us. *But we are still the ones who have to live this life and be accountable for it.* It is a mystery.

PRACTICAL SPIRIT-FILLED LIVING (Page 100)

Just because Spirit-filled living is a mystery doesn't mean we can't do it. Nothing is more practical in the growth process than to need help and empowerment in taking very difficult steps of growth.

- Julie was struggling with overeating, Ted with sexual addiction, Robbie with fear of confrontation, and I (Henry) with a strong-willed businesswoman. What did each of us learn about the Holy Spirit?

- Confession of pain, bringing things into the light from the darkness of our souls, opening up about feelings, taking risks in love and relationships, turning from what is destructive and turning to what is good, and asking God to empower us are all part of the scope of life in the Spirit. We are made to grow, to stretch ourselves into new arenas. But we are not made to do that without help.

  — When have you—like Julie, Ted, Robbie, or me—taken a step of faith and experienced the empowerment of the Holy Spirit giving you what you needed? Be specific about your feelings going into the situation as well as what happened.

  — What current circumstance is—or what upcoming situation will be—an opportunity for you to step out in faith and call on the Holy Spirit? Which step listed above (and there are many other steps) might be one step you'll have to take? Whom will you ask for prayer support when you take this step?

The Bible teaches that we are to do our part by faith and the Spirit will do his part by power. We live a real and practical life. We do not live life by summoning up willpower and strength we do not possess. Instead, we live life by summoning up faith that will be given to us by God and then stepping out on that faith.

YIELDING (Page 104)

Often in the growth process we do not know what to do, or we do not want to do what we know we should do. This is where the "control" of the Spirit comes into play, and we must yield. We must submit to what the Spirit is telling us to do and allow him to have the reins of control moment by moment (Rom. 8:9).

- The Holy Spirit talks to us, brings to mind things God has said, shows us a way out, gives us answers, gives us things to say, and pushes us to take a risk. When have you sensed the Holy Spirit doing one of these things for you? What happened?

- When the Holy Spirit nudges or reminds, our job is to yield to him and allow him to have control. We are to submit and yield our wills. How do you sense the Holy Spirit nudging you today? What will you do?

When we submit to the Holy Spirit and yield our wills to him, he takes us where we need to go, and we have taken another step of change. But sometimes we might not even know what that next step is. That's when we ask God to show us.

"SHOW ME" (Page 104)

One of the main ministries of the Holy Spirit is that he leads us to truth—the truth of God and Jesus, the illuminating truth of God's Word, the truth about people through supernatural knowledge, and the truth of situations through wisdom and prophecy. The Spirit also knows the truth of our own lives and souls, and he knows what needs to change and be revealed.

- When have you experienced the Holy Spirit leading you to truth?

- What truth would you like the Holy Spirit to reveal to you? Consider the choices above as well as specific needs in your life—and then ask him to show you the truth.

Truth is healing, and we need as much of the truth from the Holy Spirit as he will give. And that is usually as much as we are ready, able, or strong enough to receive.

WHERE HE LEADS, FOLLOW (Page 105)

Spiritual and emotional growth is a path further and further into reality. So I always try to remind people that as painful as it may be, *truth is always your friend.* No matter how difficult it is to swallow, truth is reality, and that is where ultimate safety, growth, and God are. We need to know truth.

- When has truth been a source of pain for you? Be specific.

- When have you realized, perhaps after some time had passed, that a painful truth was actually your friend? Be specific.

- Sometimes the truth leads us to what is hurting us. Sometimes it leads us to what we need to change. At other times it leads us to what we need to do next in a relationship. At still other times it leads us to what our weaknesses or limitations are. Give an example of one or two of these from your own life.

- Is truth behind any pain you are currently feeling? Who can help you see that truth as a friend?

Whatever the truth is, it is our friend. It is also where God lives. So one of the most important things God does in the process of growth is to send us his Spirit of truth. The Spirit convicts us when we are wrong, teaches us when we need it, guides us when we need to see the path, and shows us how to get there. We therefore must follow the Spirit's lead and do what he shows us to do (Gal. 5:25).

• The Holy Spirit talks to us all in different ways, as everyone's relationship with God is personal. Give an example of when the Spirit has spoken to you in one of the following ways:

> You sense the need to pray for someone who is very much on your mind.
> Something stays in your mind without you trying to think about it.
> You hear about the same issue in fifteen different contexts.
> You sense an immediate quickening of your own spirit when you hear or read or see something.

The Holy Spirit talks to us all in different ways but always with the truth we need to hear for the moment. Even though it may seem to be "bad news" at the time, it is always good news for the long haul. So listen for how he speaks to you.

• One thing is sure: The Holy Spirit can't lead past where he is leading if we don't take that first step of following him into the truth that he is showing us. God rarely shows us the whole picture at once. You see only enough light to take the very next step. As you take that one, the next one becomes clear.

— When have you experienced this gradual, step-by-step revelation of God's plan for you? Did taking those single steps of faith get any easier with each one?

— What are some reasons God might reveal his path for us just a step at a time?

— What pathway does the Holy Spirit seem to be revealing to you these days?

In the path of truth that the Holy Spirit provides, growth happens. We become more of who we truly are and begin doing what we are truly made to do.

MISCONCEPTIONS (Page 109)

Over the years we have found many misconceptions about Spirit-filled living in the Christian world of growth. Here are a few for you to watch out for.

1. If You Are "Filled with the Spirit," You Will Always Be Happy and Have No Pain or Struggle. Even Jesus felt pain. Yielding to the Spirit is something we do *in* the pain and struggle, not *instead of* the pain and struggle.

2. If You Are Filled with the Spirit, You Will Not Sin. The truth is that everyone sins. Walking in the Spirit and perfection do not mean the same thing.

3. If You Are Walking in the Spirit, You Will Have the Fruits of the Spirit Instantly. Sanctification is a process. Growth takes time.

- Which of these misconceptions has a well-meaning Christian burdened you with, which are you currently laboring under, or which have you suggested to someone else?

- What truth in this discussion of misconceptions is especially freeing to you? What will you do to start living in its light?

A WARNING (Page 110)

On the one hand, just because a person is not perfect does not mean that the Spirit is not in his life. On the other hand, if a person's life has zero evidence of light, faith, change of direction, repentance, and love, then she must ask herself if the Spirit is in her life. Either the Spirit is being quenched and not followed, or he is not even there (2 Peter 1:8–10; Gal. 5:19–25).

- What evidence of the Spirit's presence in your life can you identify? Be specific.

- If the previous question was hard to answer, ask a trusted Christian friend to point out the fruit of the Spirit in you and in your life.

No one should ever be concerned if she wishes for the Spirit's help and forgiveness, as that wish itself is a fruit of the Spirit. But showing no fruit and no concern is a different story.

IT'S NOT JUST "LET GO AND LET GOD" (Page 111)

When you preach the work of the Holy Spirit in people's lives, there is a danger. Some want to bail out of their responsibility, and they want to "let go and let God." That's not right.

- We *cannot* do the things on our own we need to do. We are *unable to make* choices on our own. We have to face our inability and depend on God. We have to depend on others. We have to reach out and be empowered. There is no "self-help."

  — When have you realized that you cannot do on your own the things you need to do?

  — What current situation is helping you realize that you cannot do on your own the things you need to do?

  — What is significant about the fact that there is no "self-help"?

- Even as we face our inability, we must take responsibility for ourselves and our life. As the Bible instructs us, we must work out our salvation—and ask God to help us do it. *It is both, not one or the other.*

  — What is the Holy Spirit's part in your growth?

  — What are your tasks in your growth? In the current situation you identified at the previous bullet?

- Describe as best you can the interaction between you working out your salvation and God helping you do so.

  — What tasks of salvation are you clearly taking responsibility for these days? Give evidence from your life.

  — What specific help are you receiving from God?

  — What tasks of salvation would you like to undertake? Who will help you? Who will hold you accountable? Who will pray for you?

  — What kind of help would you like God to provide? Ask him.

God has a part, and we have a part. Beware of dichotomizing between your tasks and God's.

SUPERNATURAL HEALING (Page 113)

In addition to the moment-by-moment work and dependency on the Holy Spirit, we can ask him to heal. I strongly believe that we can ask God to heal our own souls and can ask him to break other kinds of bondage in people's souls, such as deliverance from demonic influence or possession.

- The Bible describes God as healer and deliverer, and he heals and delivers on different timetables for different people. When have you seen God heal or deliver someone? Be specific and note the timetable he chose.

- Who is praying for you and your spiritual growth and healing—or whom might you ask to do so?

- For whom are you—or could you be—praying for healing and/or deliverance?

Prayer must be in the picture for you to have a complete picture of growth that includes God and his Holy Spirit.

NEVER TOO LATE TO BEGIN (Page 114)

I have talked to many longtime Christians who have adhered to God's principles and taught others yet have had no real life "in the Holy Spirit." If this is you, don't be dismayed, for it is never too late to begin. And the "formula" is a simple one: Just ask.

- When did you start walking "in the Spirit"? What prompted you to do that? Who introduced you to the Spirit and his very real power? What difference has walking in the Spirit made in your life?

• If you haven't yet discovered real life "in the Holy Spirit," just ask! Ask the Holy Spirit to do the things discussed in this chapter. As Jesus promised, God will give him to you (Luke 11:13).

You received Jesus in the beginning by trusting and asking. Now, in the arena of growth, do the same thing. Ask and trust. The Spirit will show up, just as Jesus promised.

Holy Spirit, thank you for the reassurance you give me about my faith and security. Thank you too for this mysterious and amazing partnership in my sanctification and growth that I want to know even better. It surely seems that I haven't been plugging into your power, so I ask you to help me, as the old hymn says, to "trust and obey." I also ask you, Holy Spirit, to show me what you want to reveal to me about my growth, my soul, and issues in my life. Show me the truth about myself as a person as well as the truth about your answers and God's ways—and then help me take the step of faith and follow you. I pray in Jesus' name. Amen.

TIPS FOR GROWERS:

• Describe your security in God and what he does through his Spirit to seek you.

• Learn more about how the Holy Spirit works, the promises God makes about his work, and the things the Holy Spirit does.

• Practice depending on the Holy Spirit by asking for help in every situation, following him, trusting in his presence with you in your pain and suffering, and calling on him for healing and deliverance.

• Ask the Holy Spirit for healing and deliverance whenever you need it.

• Remain in the paradox of both you and God living your life.

PART THREE

Finding the Best Climate

CHAPTER SEVEN

God's Plan A: People

During my own "hitting bottom" experience, I (Henry) decided to take a semester off from school, think about life, live with Bill and Julie, and "get discipled." As time went on, I could feel something changing. It was as if God were coming into view. I also found there was a lot inside of me I had never thought about. Great loads were lifted off my shoulders as I worked through hurt and forgiveness issues. And in a small group I joined, I found people could discipline me and at the same time be for me and not against me. This same community also saw in me a gift for understanding the Bible as it relates to counseling issues. Before long I knew God was calling me to go into the field of Christian counseling.

- When have you been aware—even in retrospect—of God placing exactly the right people in your life at exactly the right time? Be specific.

- When has God used people to help you see something about yourself just as Julie helped me talk about my life and my other friends saw gifts in me I hadn't noticed?

GOD USES PEOPLE TOO (Page 119)

I had wanted God to touch my depression instantaneously and heal me. Instead, he used people to help me. I came to call this God's Plan B—until I read Ephesians 4:16.

There I saw that people helping people was Plan A! The Bible said so. Not only that, but it was not *just people doing it. It was God himself!*

* When have you been aware of God healing you through people? Be specific.

* When have you been aware of God using you to bring healing to one of his children? Again, be specific.

When I studied theology in graduate school, I discovered that the doctrine of the church holds that the church, with its indwelling Spirit, is the real physical presence of Christ on earth today. God no longer lives in the temple and in the Holy of Holies. Today he lives in temples of human flesh. He lives in us, and wherever we are, he is. What an incredible reality!

THE ROLE THE BODY PLAYS IN GROWTH (Page 121)

As we talk about all the different aspects of how people grow, we want to emphasize loudly the role of the Body. Years of research and experience back up this biblical reality: *You must have relationship to grow.* Biblical growth is designed to include other people as God's instruments. To be truly biblical as well as truly effective, the growth process must include the Body of Christ. Without the Body, the process is neither totally biblical nor orthodox. So let's look briefly at some of the roles the Body plays.

* ***Connection:*** People's most basic need in life is relationship. People connected to other people thrive and grow, and those not connected wither and die.
  — The clear teaching of the New Testament is that the Body of Christ is to be people deeply connected to one another, supporting one another, and filling one another's hearts. Who are some believers you are "deeply connected to"? If you can't name anyone, what keeps you from being in intimate relationship, and what will you do to overcome those obstacles?

— As people are cut off from others and their souls are starved for connectedness, the need for love turns into an insatiable hunger for something. What have you hungrily turned to? When will you turn to God instead?

— Why does it make sense that if you don't have connection with other people in the Body, you don't have all of the connection with God you could have?

Connectedness is the foundation of how people grow. We grow first through our connection with God, but also through our connection with other people in his Body.

- **_Discipline and Structure:_** Self-discipline is always a fruit of "other-discipline." Some people are disciplined early in life and then internalize it into their character. Other people don't get disciplined early in life, and they don't ever have self-discipline until they get it from others and internalize it for themselves.

    — Would you describe yourself as "self-disciplined"? Give evidence from your life to support your answer.

    — Were you disciplined by other people when you were young? Explain.

    — What process did Jerry (page 125)—and, if your answer to the preceding question was no, what process do you—need to go through to get self-discipline?

— To whom will you turn to get the discipline process going for yourself? What schedule for meeting regularly with that person can you set up and follow? List specific tasks you and your "other(s)" will do to help discipline you.

Many times in the Bible (e.g., Matt. 18:15–16; Gal. 6:1–2; Titus 3:10) we are told that we get discipline, structure, and correction from other people whom God gives us, and we are in trouble if we do not (Prov. 15:12). So, as you try to grow in self-control over some area of life, consider the constant role of discipline.

- **Accountability:** We have already mentioned the importance of accountability, but we need to offer a caution here: *Accountability is not a cure for lack of self-control.* Accountability can expose a problem, but it can't fix it.

  — When has an accountability group or person helped you go to the agents of change you needed?

  — What current situation for potential growth might call for you to find an accountability group or person? Whom will you turn to for accountability, for seeing if you are doing the things you are supposed to be doing to solve your problem?

An accountability group or partner is not the agent of change, but that group or partner makes sure that the person being held accountable is indeed going to the agents of change.

- **Grace and Forgiveness:** By definition, grace is something we can't give ourselves. It comes from outside of us as unmerited favor. Part of the "outside" God uses to dispense his grace is other people (1 Peter 4:10). To connect fully (both head and heart) with the grace of God, we have to go to where it is, and he has chosen to put it into other people.

— When has an experience of God's grace received through his people helped you better know his grace? Describe the situation and note why you chose to open your heart to those agents of grace, your brothers and/or sisters in Christ.

— When have you confessed your sins to a fellow believer (James 5:16) and experienced God's forgiveness? Again, describe the situation and your feelings about being forgiven both before and after your confession. If you haven't ever confessed your sin to a fellow believer, what do you think is keeping you from opening your heart? Pray about that.

— What do you need to confess now? To whom will you confess—and when?

Remember Joe? *Grace can be available to us, but we might not be available to grace.* We can be around a lot of acceptance and grace, but until the hurt and guilty places of our hearts are exposed, we do not *experience* grace. So make sure that you put yourself in a place where you can be vulnerable with others. Fellowship with the depths of the heart is what heals.

• **Support and Strengthening:** Support is required throughout the growth process. We will face tasks and realties past our strength and abilities, so we need others to support us (1 Thess. 5:14; Gal. 6:2). Support enables people to go through grief, trials, growth, and a whole host of other difficult times.

— What difficult seasons in your life have been made easier by support from other people? Note the type and/or source of support you experienced.

— When have you been able to offer support to someone going through tough times?

— Explain in your own words how healing in the Body of Christ parallels healing in the physical body (pages 132–33).

— What current set of circumstances in your life might be easier to deal with if you let yourself be vulnerable and turn to God's people for support? What kind of support do you need? How will you structure that support? To whom will you turn for support—and when? And who will hold you accountable for reaching out for that support?

The Body has myriad gifts, and as a person is exposed to all the ingredients of growth in that Body, the infection is healed. This is the way God designed it. This is Plan A.

MENTORING THE WHOLE PERSON (Page 133)

Sometimes we think of mentoring only in terms of one's professional life, but mentoring is for all of the different roles in life. You might need mentoring as a mother or father, as a wife or husband. Or you might need to be a spiritual leader to someone in your life. Mentoring equips you for whatever God has called you to do in your current situation. After all, God wants us to develop all of our gifts and talents, not just our "spiritual" ones. We often see spiritual growth as affecting only those parts of life that relate to God, like prayer, Bible study, and worship. We do not see growth in our work and career as spiritual growth. Yet, in reality, all of life belongs to God, and the Bible speaks to all of it (Prov. 27:23–26, for example).

- When have you been mentored? Describe the focus, the results, and the relationship. Consider whether or not it fostered the all-too-common split between work (or "real life") and spiritual life.

- When have you mentored someone? What was the focus? Did you try to integrate the "spiritual" into work or "real life"? If so, what did you do?

- Does being mentored seem like a good idea at this point in your life? Make this possibility a topic of prayer. Ask God to reveal, first, if a mentor is his plan for you right now and, second, how you might connect with a mentor who can see what is happening in your overall walk of faith and growth in Christ. Where might you find a possible mentor? Where will you go to put yourself in a position where God can bring you and a potential mentor together?

We should provide mentoring in all aspects of life as part of spiritual growth in the Body, and then we would not only see people achieve more success, but also see them resolve the split between their spiritual and professional lives. Even those people such as stay-at-home moms or fast-food workers, whose jobs are not technically "professional," can learn to see their jobs as essentially spiritual.

GRIEVING (Page 135)

One of the most important processes in life is grief. God has designed grief to help us get over things. When bad things happen in life, we have to work through them: we walk through the experience, take it in, use what is useful, and eliminate the waste.

- What experiences of grief, what loss or injury, have you had? What role did you let the community of believers play in your grieving process?

- Grief can only be accomplished in relationship. What does this suggest about whether you have grieved sufficiently for the events you just listed?

- When has God used you to help another person grieve? What did you learn— about grief, the Holy Spirit, God's plan for his Body, or something else—from that experience?

- Review the discussion of grief. What has kept you from doing the grieving you need to do? Where will you get the resources you need to grieve, and when will you take that step? With whom will you grieve, and who will hold you accountable for fully griev-ing your loss?

The only way grief can happen well is in relationship—the way God designed it to work. Grieve correctly—*with other people*—and you can get on with life.

HEALING (Page 137)

We deal with the specifics of healing the brokenhearted in chapter 14, but here we have to mention that it occurs within the Body. Relationships provide care, support, structure, and the balm of love to heal hurts.

- What hurts of rejection, abuse, abandonment, or something else have wounded your soul? Where have you turned for healing? If you turned to the Body of Christ, describe what happened. If you turned elsewhere, comment on the sufficiency of the healing.

- When have you seen the Body of Christ lancing, holding, medicating, and protecting—healing—the hurts of one of its members? Be specific about the process as well as the outcome.

- Review the discussion of healing. What has kept you from receiving the healing you need? What will help you face your pain? Who will help you heal, and who will hold you accountable for staying with the healing process?

If hurts are deeply healed, people do not repeat these hurts in other relationships, nor do they try to medicate their wounds in sinful ways. If the Body is the medicine—the medicine that heals, not just dulls the pain—then the destructive cycle of sin is broken.

CONFRONTING, CONTAINING SIN, ADMINISTERING TRUTH (Page 137)

Part of the role of the Body is to step in and contain the effects of sin in someone's life. The Body is sometimes an "antibody"; its role is to fight infection (Gal. 6:1).

- What was striking about the intervention in Michael's life and the results?

- When have you been involved in an intervention? Comment on why it was necessary, how it was handled, and what it accomplished.

- Whom do you need to confront? What is keeping you from doing so? What will you do to find the courage to confront that person? What do you want that confrontation to look like? When and where will you confront that person? Who will pray for you as well as hold you accountable for confronting the person in love and administering God's truth? Pray about these various aspects of the situation.

The role of the Body is to intervene—as in Michael's situation—and save people from the destruction in which they find themselves. But the key is how it is done. When you confront, make sure you are doing it Jesus' way, speaking the very words of God (1 Peter 4:11) and doing so in a spirit of gentleness (Gal. 6:1).

MODELING (Page 140)

We cannot do what we have never seen done. We need models to show us how (1 Thess. 1:6–7; 1 John 2:6). God designed humans with a need to see others first do what they need to learn and then internalize that modeling and be able to repeat it.

- What healthy behavior have you seen modeled so that you could learn it? Be specific about both the modeling and your efforts to imitate that model.

- What wrong modeling have you had to renounce?

- Consider prayerfully what modeling you are offering those closest to you. Ask the Holy Spirit to show you any behaviors and attitudes you need to change—and then, by his power, make the necessary changes.

- For what aspects of life do you need to see some good modeling? Where and when will you go to find these models? Who will hold you accountable to seek and find those good models you need?

As Paul said, we imitate those who imitate Christ. His Body carries on his walk on the earth, and others learn it.

UNIVERSALITY OF IMPERFECTION AND SUFFERING
(Page 141)

To find out that others—even successful people—struggle reduces our shame, fear, and guilt and gives us hope as well as models of how to cope. We also see that we don't have to have it all together to be followers of Christ.

• When have you experienced some relief upon finding out that someone you respected and who appeared so "together" also struggles?

• Which of the following have you experienced as a result of learning that other people struggle? Give details about each benefit.

  Feeling less guilty, ashamed, and afraid something is wrong with you.

  Obtaining a more accurate view of the standard you are trying to live up to.

  Gaining hope and problem-solving skills.

• With whom in your life are you able to be open about your struggles—and therefore able to experience the three benefits mentioned above?

• If you aren't close enough to people to either hear about their struggles or share your own, what do you think God wants you to do? To what safe place can you go, for instance, to hear about the struggles of others, share your own, and be reassured that you are not the only one who has issues to resolve? Who will hold you accountable for taking that step?

While we all have different struggles, one thing is certain: We all struggle. And the knowledge that we are not alone on our path of struggle is one of the best things the Body can give one another. No one is exempt; therefore no one needs to be ashamed of not having it all together.

DISCIPLESHIP (Page 143)

The value of discipleship cannot be overestimated. In this context, doctrine can be passed on in a personal way as it relates to real life. Questions can be asked, sin confessed, and accountability offered. Encouragement can be integrated into the spiritual learning process. In short, faith development becomes a relational process where personal development and faith intertwine in an organic way.

- What has been your view of discipleship? Has it seemed too rigorous, too rigid, too religious? Something else? In light of what you've learned in this book, what do you see as the value of discipleship?

- When have you been discipled or a discipler? Talk about your experience(s).

- We encourage discipleship as a function of the Body for everyone, in two directions: Who in your life might disciple you, and whom might you disciple? Pray about some possibilities and a course of action. What step will you take toward being discipled? When will you take it? What step will you take toward discipling someone else? When will you take it? Who will hold you accountable for both being discipled and discipling?

How beautiful it would be if everyone could experience what Paul said of his work with others and then pass it on to others: "For you know that we dealt with each of you as a father deals with his own children, encouraging, comforting and urging you to live lives worthy of God, who calls you into his kingdom and glory" (1 Thess. 2:11–12).

A COMPLETE MAKEOVER (Page 145)

Throughout this book you will notice the role of the Body threaded through every task. The Bible teaches that growth happens in the Body of Christ as he imparts his gifts to each member.

• The theology of redemption is not one of rehabilitation; it is one of total destruction, of starting all over again, at *birth*. We are not to be "improved"; we are to be crucified and *born again*. As Paul says, the old has been crucified, and all things have become new (2 Cor. 5:17; Gal. 2:20). In what areas of your life have you felt—or do you feel—like a child who is learning (1 John 2:12–14), a new-born babe (1 Peter 2:2), or an infant (Heb. 5:13)?

• None of us has made it to adulthood "complete," for we all came from a dysfunctional family: the human race. We have to go through a rebirth and a re-growing up, this time in a new family—his family, the Body of Christ.

— What are you experiencing and receiving from your new family, the Body of Christ, that you didn't experience and receive before? Some possibilities are nurturance, modeling, truth, love, accountability, and the development of your talents. Be specific.

— What do you need to receive from this new family? Whom will you ask for those things? What will you do to put yourself in a position where you can receive those things?

— Growing up to maturity and completeness is all about character development, the process of sanctification. What is new, exciting, and even empowering about the fact that these three phrases—"growing up to maturity and completeness," "character development," and "the process of sanctification"—are profoundly related to one another?

- Proverbs 13:20 says, "He who walks with the wise grows wise, but a companion of fools suffers harm."

  — Are you walking and spending time with good people? Support your "yes" with specific evidence of someone's positive influence on your growth.

  — What wise person will you try to "walk with"? What will you do to initiate that relationship—and when? Who will hold you accountable for taking that step toward connection?

  — God's pattern has always been about life giving life. As he breathed life into humankind, and as that life is passed on from one person to another, so is spiritual and personal growth. It is produced in one and passed on to another. When have you seen—or, ideally, experienced—this pattern, both the giving and receiving of spiritual and personal growth? Be specific about *what* was passed on and *how* it was passed on.

  — In what current situation are you both giving and receiving spiritual and personal growth? Be specific about the circumstances and the growth you're sensing.

Make sure you are in a Body that is growing you up. That's doing it according to Plan A.

Lord God, thank you for the ways you use your people, the Body of Christ, as channels of your grace. It's through your people that I can experience grace with my heart and not just know about it in my head.

So please show me when I need to turn to your Body for growth—for connection and accountability, discipline and structure, grace and forgiveness, support and strengthening; for mentoring, grieving, and healing; or for confronting sin and administering truth. Also, I ask, show me the steps I need to take to experience this growth in your Body. And please provide me with people who will help me grow and guide me to the places where growth can happen. Help me to seek what you have for me. Help me to knock—and then please open those doors to growth as I step out in faith. In Jesus' name. Amen.

TIPS FOR GROWERS:

- Examine your feelings about Plan A. Evaluate how comfortable you are with God's using people to accomplish what he wants to do in your life. Then consider whether you are fitting into Plan A: Determine whether you are connected to the community of believers, which is God's provision for you, or whether you have amputated yourself from the body of Christ.

- Take an inventory in your life and give an example of when you have received any of these things the body provides:

  —Connection

  —Discipline and structure

  —Accountability

  —Grace and forgiveness

  —Support and strengthening

  —Mentoring

  —Grieving

  —Modeling

  —Healing

  —Confronting

- Determine whether you experience the universality of suffering and imperfection by being closely connected to other people.

- Figure out whether you have ever been personally discipled or need to be.

- Start thinking of spiritual growth as a total makeover and growing up again in a new family, the family of God. Find a community that will provide these elements.

CHAPTER EIGHT

Open Spaces: The Power of Acceptance

The night that Gary confessed his affair with my (John's) small group was one of the milestones on his spiritual journey—and it shifted the entire nature of our group. We started discussing life and God in more vulnerable and open ways. Gary's openness tore down our fears of being vulnerable and mended deep places within all of us. I learned much about the good things that happen in our hearts when we feel accepted.

IT STARTS WITH GOD (Page 149)

The Bible teaches that acceptance begins with God: "Accept one another, then, just as Christ accepted you, in order to bring praise to God" (Rom. 15:7). Christ's acceptance of us is the model for how we are to accept one another.

- Acceptance is the state of receiving someone into relationship. To be accepted is to have all of your parts, good and bad, received by another without condemnation. It is closely related to grace, undeserved merit. Acceptance is the result of the working of grace.

  — Who in your life has offered you the gift of acceptance, receiving all of your parts, good and bad, without condemnation?

  — Who in your life has been encouraged by your acceptance of his/her parts, good and bad?

— Where are you getting total acceptance in your life now? If you can't identify any sources of such acceptance, why not? What's getting in the way? What will you do to find acceptance—and when will you take the first step?

• God originally designed acceptance as a way of life. As humans, we were to relate to him and to one another with no thought of condemnation, judgment, or criticism. When we sinned and fell from grace, God in his holy nature could not accept our sinfulness, yet his love kept him caring for us. So God provided a costly solution: His Son Jesus—fully God, fully man, and without sin—died to atone for our sins (1 Peter 3:18).

— Think back to when you first heard this gospel truth. What difference in your life does being accepted by God make?

— Do you know someone who feels unacceptable? Pray for an opportunity to share the gospel truth with that person. Ask the Holy Spirit to prepare that person to hear the message and to guide your timing as well as your thoughts and words when you meet.

• God's acceptance of us in no way negates or minimizes our badness. He receives us now not because we are innocent, but because our debt of guilt has been fully paid once and for all.

— Is there a sin in your life that you think God can't or won't forgive? Make this a topic of Bible study, prayer, and confession so that you can come to know God's forgiveness and acceptance. The Bible teaches that if you confess your sin, God will forgive you (1 John 1:9). Nothing is unforgivable except blasphemy against the Spirit, which is the final rejection of Christ (Matt. 12:31). If you accept Jesus as your Savior and Lord, nothing you think, say, or do is unforgivable.

— God calls us to confess our sin to one another (James 5:16). If you've ever done that, describe the experience. Comment on what that person's acceptance of you after your confession helped you realize about God's forgiveness and acceptance of you. Or if you have never confessed your sin to a fellow believer, consider whether doing so might be not only an act of obedience, but a way God can free you from troublesome feelings of being unforgiven or unforgivable. To whom will you confess your sin, and when will you do so?

When we are afraid that God will not accept us because we have done something wrong, it is we who, at some level, are negating and minimizing what he has done for us. There is truly no condemnation for those who belong to Jesus (Rom. 8:1).

WHAT ACCEPTANCE DOES IN GROWTH (Page 149)

Acceptance plays many roles in how people grow. It is central to the process.

- **Acceptance Frees from Bondage to the Law:** Acceptance breaks our bondage to the impossible demands of the law, which have been fulfilled in Jesus (Matt. 5:17). Acceptance does away with the need to prove ourselves worthy by performance and good works, and we become free to concentrate on love and growth.

  — What are you doing to try to make yourself good enough for God and/or other people?

  — Why won't you stop trying to earn people's acceptance?

- **Acceptance Builds Trust and Relationship:** Relationship and growth can't occur unless both knowledge and love are present. Acceptance bridges the gap between being known and being loved.

— With whom can you be "careless," not needing to edit every word you say, not walking on eggshells, and not pretending to be someone you're not?

— If you don't yet know this kind of acceptance, pray about it. Ask God to guide you to a safe group of people and to give you the courage to let yourself be known — and accepted.

- ***Acceptance Provides Healing and Growth in and of Itself:*** The warmth of acceptance and the permission to be ourselves allow us to bring to light parts of ourselves that need to be connected to relationship. This connection to relationship fuels growth in us.

  — When has a person's "being there" for you meant more than any sage advice that might have been offered instead?

  — Who is "being there" for you right now? If no one is there for you right now, where will you go to find such an important person?

- ***Acceptance Creates Safety to Be and Experience Ourselves:*** We need to experience all of our souls, whether good, bad, or broken. Otherwise, what is not brought into the light of God's love and relationship cannot be matured, healed, and integrated into the rest of our character.

  — When have you lived your life as if struggles, failures, depression, sad times, addictions, or neediness didn't exist — or are you doing so now?

— When has being accepted brought to light your needs, your sins, parts of you that you don't like or accept, your hiding styles, or your brokenness and weakness? Explain why such bringing into the light is both hard and good at the same time.

— With whom are you able to be yourself? If no one in your life gives you that kind of acceptance, what will you do to find someone who will?

• **Acceptance Creates Safety to Confess and Heal:** To experience and "be" our sinful or broken selves is only one step in spiritual growth. Another necessary step is to bring those feelings and parts into relationship with God and others (James 5:16). The Bible calls this step "confession," meaning "to agree with the truth."

— When have you risked sharing a negative part of yourself with someone? Talk about that experience.

— What aspect or aspects of yourself need to be brought into the light (see Eph. 5:8–14)? With whom will you share that part of you?

• **Acceptance Increases Initiative and Risk in Growth:** Acceptance often starts "movement" in someone's spiritual growth. As acceptance increases, so does confession, and with confession come intimacy and growth. After all, when you know that risking won't bring judgment, you can try new things.

— Explain in your own words why acceptance can spark progress in someone's spiritual growth.

— What new thing(s) would you try if you knew you wouldn't be judged?

• Take your temperature! Truly healthy people know they have good parts and bad parts. List two or three of your good parts and two or three of your bad parts.

Healthy people also have the acceptance and grace to deal with their bad parts in God's process of growth.

ACCEPTING ACCEPTANCE: FOR THE GROWER (Page 155)

If you are growing, several things can help you find greater acceptance from God and others. Often we don't know what to do with acceptance, or we are afraid of it. The following steps will help you on your path to maturity.

• **Be Aware of Your Need:** Acceptance is meaningless if there is nothing that needs to be accepted. So take the humble step of confessing your lacks and needs to God and to others. Note those lacks and needs here.

• **Give Up the Law as a Means to Acceptance:** We want to earn love and acceptance. It helps us think we are in control. Ask God to show you your tendencies to work for acceptance from him or from others. Also consider whether you are working hard in life because you are already accepted or because you want acceptance. Explain.

• **Deal with Tendencies to Negate Acceptance:** Be honest with yourself: What are you doing to push away acceptance? And why are you doing so?

- *Use Acceptance to Grow:* Are you content merely to be accepted or seek acceptance? Think about what growth can happen in you once you are both known and loved, once you are accepted. Jot down a few possibilities here.

- *Request, Don't Demand It:* Never forget that acceptance is entirely a gift from God and others. (In actuality, each of us deserves death [Ezek. 18:4]).

  — In what ways or with whom are you trying to demand acceptance? When has someone tried to demand you to accept her? Describe your response.

  — Are you trying to demand acceptance from someone? What would your request for acceptance look like and/or sound like?

- *Don't Confuse Acceptance with Agreement:* While some criticism can be judgmental, direct loving criticism is a necessary part of spiritual growth. In fact, where there is no confrontation, growth is seriously hampered (Eph. 4:15).

  — When have you confused honest feedback with judgment? When have you experienced the reality that the truth hurts, but it heals?

  — What confrontation are you avoiding? Whose honest feedback are you discounting or even avoiding?

CREATING A CONTEXT FOR ACCEPTANCE: FOR THE HELPER (Page 157)

It is difficult to create an accepting environment in which people open up, give up the law, and confess. Here are some ways to foster acceptance in a growth group.

- ***Let People Know That Acceptance Is the Norm.***
  — What will you say to let your group know that condemnation and judgment will not be acceptable?

  — What evidence from the Bible will you use to explain that acceptance is the way God treats us and therefore it is the way we are to treat others?

- ***Be Vulnerable.***
  — Which of your own failings might be appropriate to share?

  — What personal example(s) of being accepted could you tell the group about?

- ***Deal with Acceptance Problems as Internal Issues.***
  — When have you seen a judgmental person judging in someone else an aspect of his own soul that he can't tolerate?

— Think through what you will say to a judgmental member of your group who needs to investigate what he might be reacting to inside.

- ### *Distinguish Between the Sin and the Sinner.*
    — What can you say to make a person see that you are confronting her about sin, not judging her?

    — What will you do and say to extend to her the grace of acceptance before you confront her?

- ### *Maintain a Humble Stance Toward Growth.*
    — What will you say if you need to confront spiritual nonacceptance, a person's sense that she can't relate to others in her life because they are now in two different worlds?

    — What will you say to explain, first, that growth is a gift from God and, second, that as we are accepted at deeper levels, we are to accept others in our lives even more fully?

- ***Keep a Process Orientation to Acceptance.***

  — Think about your own process of accepting people and receiving acceptance from others. What was your timetable, and what were your struggles?

  — What will you do to help someone tolerate what he or she can bear right here and now—and then nudge that person toward further acceptance?

The safety of acceptance promotes spiritual growth. In the next chapter we deal with an obstacle to acceptance: condemnation.

Lord God, it is a sign of your amazing grace that you accept me, all of me, the good parts and the bad, on my good days and on my bad ones. Thank you—and thank you that you want me to learn both to receive acceptance from other people and to extend acceptance to those in my life. Please help me be patient with the process and grant me courage for the healing that can result as I confront my needs, my sins, the parts of me I've never liked or accepted, those aspects of me that I hide, my brokenness, and my weakness. I don't want to be afraid of the truth. I want to trust you to use it to heal me. And I thank you in advance for what you have for me. In Jesus' name. Amen.

TIPS FOR GROWERS:

- Define what the Bible means by *acceptance*. Be aware of any tendencies to see acceptance either as negating our true badness or as being based on our goodness, neither of which is real acceptance.

- Take an inventory of how acceptance or its lack has affected your life. For example, why has being with unaccepting people kept you from opening up to grace? In what ways has resisting the acceptance of God and others kept you disconnected from growth? In what ways has genuine acceptance helped you grow?

- Investigate what specific parts of your soul exist outside of acceptance. Find out both why they do and what you can do to bring them to acceptance.

CHAPTER NINE

The Warmth of the Sun: Forgiveness

We have talked to many people who ask God for his forgiveness, receive it, and then find they cannot feel it. In this chapter we will look at the causes of guilt and how the spiritual growth process can resolve them. We will look at where guilt comes from, some misconceptions about dealing with it, and what works.

THE SOURCE AND RESOLUTION OF GUILT (Page 163)

Remember the discussion of the Fall in chapter 2 and look again at the discussion on pages 163–65. This review will help you understand how our guilt is resolved.

- Explain in your own words the gospel truth of what God did to resolve our guilt.

- What statements in Romans 8:33–39 are especially meaningful to you?

Guilt came from being separated from God, and guilt can be resolved by being reconnected to God through Jesus. We go from guilty to not guilty by believing. This is the theology of guilt in the Christian faith. A "guilty Christian" is an oxymoron.

TWO SIDES, TWO EXPERIENCES (Page 165)

But many Christians still feel guilty. The problem is that our hearts can condemn us even when God does not (1 John 3:20; 4:18). So we have to ask, "What are the conditions inside of us that prevent us from feeling forgiveness even when we are surely forgiven?" Let's look at some of the answers.

- **Wrong Teaching:** Wrong teaching or incomplete knowledge of what the Bible says can keep us from feeling forgiven. You may just not know.

  — What does the Bible really say about forgiveness and God's grace?

  Psalm 103:12

  Romans 3:22

  Romans 7:1

  Romans 8:33–39

  Hebrews 10:1–3

  1 John 1:9

  — Memorize one or two of the passages listed above.

  — You can only receive God's forgiveness to the degree you are confessing your sin. What sin do you need to confess? Do so now.

If confession is taking place, God will cleanse and purify us (1 John 1:9).

- ***Disconnection from Grace:*** James says, "Therefore confess your sins to each other and pray for each other so that you may be healed" (James 5:16). As we do that, we internalize from each other the grace we need.

  — You can't fix something that's under the attack of guilt. What part of you are you feeling guilty about and therefore cutting yourself off from the healing grace available through God and his people? With whom will you share that part of you so that you can receive God's healing grace? When will you do so? If you aren't sure whom to turn to, where will you go to find a safe person—and when?

  — Based on our past relationships, we learn how to accept or reject ourselves. What have your past relationships taught you? Be specific.

  — Explain in your own words why part of the answer for people who reject themselves is joining a supportive, accepting community.

  — Are you someone who might benefit greatly from being part of a group of accepting people? Will you seek one out? Why or why not?

  When all of our badness is known—and loved by grace—it loses its power. The goal is for grace to know all of our bad parts, and confession to God and others achieves that. The result is that guilt is dissolved.

- ***False Standards:*** People who grow up with unrealistic standards from their parents, the media, or the culture often have an "ideal" person in their head to which they compare themselves, and the result is relentless guilt or shame.

— What do you tell yourself about how you "should" be acting, feeling, thinking, growing, working, parenting, and succeeding? Be specific.

— What standards are you measuring yourself against?

— Where did those standards come from? (Consider them in light of Psalm 103:13–14.)

Community gets us more in touch with reality and therefore with our false standards. Community also helps us see failure as normal.

- **Weak Conscience:** A weak conscience can keep us from feeling forgiven. The Bible defines "weak conscience" as one that is too strict and is confused on the issues of right and wrong. Sometimes a weak conscience can convict people of things that are not even real issues (1 Cor. 8:7–12).

  — When have you known someone who was feeling convicted about something that wasn't even a real issue? Describe the situation.

  — Are you now feeling convicted about something that may not be a real issue—or have you ever felt convicted about something that proved not to be a real issue? Explain the situation. If it is current, what will you do to determine whether or not the issue is real? If you're thinking about a past situation, what happened to help you realize that the issue was not really important? What role did God's people play in your realization?

If people feel guilty for things that are not even issues, they need the safety and grace of an accepting environment—first, to find out what the Bible really teaches, and, second, to face their own appetites and impulses.

- *Idealization of Conscience:* An issue related to weak conscience is the idealization of conscience, which can also keep us from feeling forgiven. When people think that just feeling bad about something means they really are bad, they might be blindly accepting what their conscience says. In other words, they think their conscience is ideal, or without flaw.

  — When have you blindly accepted what your conscience said to you? What thoughts and behaviors followed?

  — Do you find yourself falling into this category: "People who never question what they feel and think"? What might be behind such an approach to life? If you are one who doesn't question your feelings and thoughts, who might help you learn to do so?

As the apostle Paul says, his conscience could very well be wrong, and it is God who judges us (1 Cor. 4:4).

- *Confusion of Conscience with the Holy Spirit:* A person can feel guilty about something and say, "The Holy Spirit is convicting me." This person equates guilt feelings with the voice of the Holy Spirit. The guilt is the person's feeling; a conviction of the Holy Spirit is something he says and does. It is his imparting of the truth to us.

  — Based on this discussion (page 171 of the text) and what you know from Scripture, what are some guidelines for determining whether the Holy Spirit is convicting you about something?

— Why is guilt not necessarily a sign that the Holy Spirit is trying to teach you something?

— Are you currently ignoring the Holy Spirit's attempts to teach you or guide you? Explain your answer.

People may feel guilt when the Holy Spirit points something out, but this guilt is not the Holy Spirit's doing. If people feel guilt in response to the Spirit's voice, they have not yet realized that they are not condemned for what he is pointing out.

• **Godly Sorrow Versus Worldly Sorrow:** The Bible says we should not feel guilty, but we should feel sorry. There is a big difference: Guilt focuses on me. It focuses on how bad I am, not on what I have done to hurt you. Godly sorrow, however, focuses on the offended party. Those who express godly sorrow empathize with how their behavior has affected someone else.

— Which has characterized your life more—godly sorrow or worldly sorrow? Offer some examples from your life.

— Explain why guilt is about the law and godly sorrow is about love.

— What worldly sorrow are you currently dealing with? Put differently, what are you feeling guilty about? Take a step toward godly sorrow by considering how the behavior you're feeling guilty about has affected someone else.

Get off the guilt and onto how your behavior affects other people. This is love.

THE NATURE OF CORRECTION (Page 173)

Our conscience makes us aware of right and wrong, and when we violate a standard, it corrects us. Conscience, however, can be flawed in many ways. For instance, it can be wrong in its corrective tone.

*   What tone of voice does your conscience have when it points out a violation?

*   If the tone of your conscience is one of grace and truth, thank God for the blessing of an inner voice that is not only honest but also kind and accepting. Also ask him where he might use you to help transform someone's conscience from an enemy to a friend.

*   If the tone of your conscience is harsh and angry, where can you go to find people who will speak grace and truth with kindness and acceptance so that you can internalize their voices? If you're not sure, pray about it.

A group can do for you what Summer's group did for her. It won't call you stupid and be angry with you. Its tone will be "for" you. This is what grace is, and such grace can transform your conscience from an enemy into a friend.

TRUE GUILT AND FALSE GUILT (Page 175)

No one should feel bad about things that are not bad. That would be "false guilt." On the other hand, when we commit an offense, we are guilty of committing that offense. But this does not mean that our proper response is to feel guilty and condemned. Instead, we should feel "godly sorrow," which, as we have seen, focuses on the other person.

*   From the Bible's perspective, guilt is not even a problem. Jesus died to end that problem, once and for all, so that we could deal with the real problems in our lives

and souls. Forget the guilt and solve the problems, because if you don't, you are going to reap death.

— What kind of guilt are you carrying around?

— Trevor was plagued with guilt that kept him from dealing with his problems (pages 176–77). What problems might your guilt be keeping you from dealing with?

Condemnation has no place, but serious worry about sin does. Guilt does nothing to help one stop sinning, but getting a picture of what sin is doing to one's life does. Guilt is not the issue; sin is.

- **_Guilt as an Old Voice:_** Any aspect of our selves that is disapproved of or attacked in a significant relationship can come under "judgment," and then guilt attacks that part of the soul from the inside.

    — What aspects of yourself were disapproved of or attacked? Consider these:

Needs	Strength
Anger	Separateness
Talents	Pain
Success	Failures
Independence	Sexuality
Weaknesses	Honesty
Sadness	Autonomy

— What kind of voice in your conscience has this disapproval resulted in?

Many times people have to express themselves in new, safe relational settings to get the healing and encouragement God provides to restore the soul. A new conscience has to be internalized and developed in new relationships. Again the Body of Christ does that work.

- *Anger:* Anger is one aspect of the self that can be paired with guilt messages. Anger is a state of protest and fight. It is a problem-solving emotion designed to protect what is good and what is valuable.

    — But sometimes people have not expressed anger toward bad things that have happened to them because doing so would have been dangerous. So they deny their anger. When have you denied your feelings of anger? Explain. What prompted you to realize that you were in denial about your anger?

    — Child abuse, hurtful parenting, and other oppressive relationships prompt people to turn the anger that should be aimed at the abuser toward themselves. What evidence do you see of your anger being turned inward on yourself? Consider your feelings, behavior, words, level of patience, and the intensity and appropriateness of your reaction when something doesn't go your way. What might be a more appropriate way to handle your anger?

    — Are you laboring under a sense that you're not forgiven for something? If so, whom will you talk to for help with resolving this issue?

— What anger are you carrying these days? What will you do about it? To whom will you turn for the support (prayers, listening, accountability) you need? When will you take the first step?

Be careful of a misdiagnosis. Many people suffer for a long time at the hands of others trying to get them to "believe" they are forgiven when what they should be working on is the resolution of their anger.

THE CHILD POSITION (Page 181)

Sometimes guilt is not a problem to be solved; instead, it is a symptom of the one-down child position from which these people experience peers as parental figures who will approve or judge them.

- When do you feel "one-down" to others? Why do you have that feeling? Or why not?

- Skills like being assertive, being honest, embracing sexuality, taking risks with talents, thinking for oneself, and separating from one's parents are all essential to coming out from under the child position. How well are you doing/have you done in each of these areas? What course of action does your answer suggest to you?

Again, the issue here is that the problem is not always the problem. Guilt was never the issue. Guilt was just a symptom of a person who had never grown up, and the task is to grow up.

ISOLATION (Page 182)

Guilt is basically about separation from love (1 John 4:18). If people know they are loved, they are not afraid of their "badness."

- If you are feeling bad about yourself, the answer is never to get you to feel better about yourself. Since feelings of badness are a symptom of the basic problem of our disconnection from love, the answer is to get you connected to love.

  — When do you feel bad about yourself?

  — What are you doing to try to make yourself feel "better" about yourself? How well is that method working?

  — In what ways are you trying to overcome isolation by performing "better"? Are your efforts paying off?

  — People who feel "bad" about themselves are disconnected from love. What part of your heart is isolated from people who could love you?

  — Where might you go to receive the grace, love, and connection that can cure guilt?

- Take a moment to think about the people in your life.

  — What person comes to mind when you think about someone feeling "bad" about himself or herself?

— What might you do to connect to the isolated part of that person's heart?

— What form of grace, love, and connection might be meaningful to that person? Be prayerful and let God use you.

An alone self is a bad self. If someone feels alone, he or she is going to feel "bad." The answer is not "goodness," or more self-esteem, or positive affirmations. The answer is love.

THE GOOD NEWS (Page 184)

Jesus said that he did not come into the world to judge or condemn it (John 12:47).

- The Bible teaches that there should be no guilt for the Christian. Explain why.

- Instead, there should be the freedom of "no condemnation" along with a deep concern for real problems and issues. Who has extended this grace and love to you — and to whom can you extend it today?

Remember that guilt is not a problem, but a symptom of being separated from Love. The solution to this problem is always reconciliation to Love. It is simple yet sometimes very difficult—but as the apostle Paul tells us, it "never fails" (1 Cor. 13:8).

Lord God, thank you that there is no condemnation for us who have named Jesus as our Savior and Lord! Thank you that you have freed us from guilt—and please help me to receive this amazing gift from you. Show me what keeps me from knowing the freedom from guilt that you desire for your children. Please also reveal to me any anger I need to resolve and any relationship in which I have given someone the position of God-the-parent. I ask you, Lord, to help me experience love rather than isolation, and use me to share that kind of love with others. Finally, I thank you that your love never fails. In Jesus' precious name. Amen.

TIPS FOR GROWERS:

- Review your understanding of guilt and see if it squares with what the Bible teaches. Note also whether there is a disconnect between what your head believes about guilt and what your heart experiences. If so, determine why.

- The real problem of guilt is not bad feelings or being bad, but separation. Identify any ways your guilt keeps you separated from God, his grace, love, and other people. Consider also what is continuing to keep you separated from these good and healing things.

- Examine where these causes of pathological guilt are operating in your life:
  False standards
  Weak conscience
  Strict background
  Idealization of conscience
  Worldly sorrow versus godly sorrow
  The tone of your correction
  True guilt versus false guilt issues
  Not seeing the real issues that are the problem
  Old voices
  Resolving anger
  The child position
  Isolation

- Determine what contexts and activities with God and others can help reverse the separation from love you are experiencing and provide the healing you need.

PART FOUR

The Path of Growth

CHAPTER TEN

The Gardener's Handbook: The Bible

"When my boyfriend does a lot of cocaine, he beats me up. What am I supposed to do?" As a seminary student, all I (John) could muster was a paraphrase of Romans 8:28, and I knew I hadn't really helped Cindy. The problem was how I viewed the Bible's work in the lives of people. I believed and practiced the biblical disciplines of study, reading, memorization, prayer, commitment, and surrender. But I had an incomplete idea of how the Bible addresses the spiritual growth process.

* What do you think you would have said to Cindy?

* When have you found your knowledge of the Bible inadequate?

* Which of the following biblical disciplines have been a helpful and regular part of your life: study, reading, memorization, prayer, commitment, and surrender? Which of these disciplines will you work on strengthening this week?

As I studied, I found that the Bible is complete. It contains all the principles we need to understand for both growing spiritually and resolving personal struggles. And it asserts the same theology I had learned in school, but now I saw this theology in light of God's process of growing his people. This chapter talks about the specific and unique part the Bible plays in the growth process.

THE POWER OF THE WORD (Page 191)

Reading the Bible is one of the main ways God speaks to our lives and hearts. Although learning principles and truths is very important, coming close to God personally through the Bible is a higher value (Ps. 119:27).

- ***The Bible Points to God as the Source of All Growth:*** The Bible anchors God as the source of all growth. All the way through the Bible we read that everything we need in life comes from him, not from ourselves (Acts 17:28; 1 Cor. 4:7). This essential and defining reality helps to humble us and make us dependent on God. And when we see that the Bible points to God for all growth, we understand that all growth is spiritual growth.

  — Think about your growth as an individual. When have you taken credit for it? Looking back now, what evidence of God's fingerprints do you see on it?

  — In what aspect(s) of your life are you not yet fully dependent on God? What act of humbling might it take before you depend more on him? Perhaps a reading of Psalm 119 could save you some pain.

  — Hurting people need relationship and love as well as God's Word for comfort and healing. When have you received the prescription "Get into the Word"? What was your reaction to that advice?

— If you are hurting now, what passages of the Bible and what relationships are offering you comfort? If you don't have a good balance, find a resource to guide you through Scripture or a place where you can find relationship with safe people.

• ***The Bible Prescribes the Path of Growth:*** The Bible clearly presents a process for pursuing spiritual maturity. It refers to the process in different ways, such as sanctification, transformation, and growth. At heart, the idea is that we are designed to become increasingly more of who we were created to be (2 Cor. 3:18).

— *The elements:* The Scriptures teach that relationship, truth, and time must be present for growth. Are you in relationship with God? Who and what are the sources of truth in your life? Have you seen growth in yourself over time?

— *The tasks:* In addition to the traditional disciplines of Bible study and prayer, the hard and sometimes painful work of growth involves the following:

Submission and obedience to God (Rom. 12:1)

Need and dependency (Prov. 3:5–6)

Responsibility and ownership (Luke 9:23)

Forgiveness (Matt. 6:12–15)

When have you seen a connection between these tasks and growth? Ask God to show you the task(s) you need to tackle—and then tackle them!

— *The resources:* God is the ultimate Source of all we need, but his Creation is a resource of good things. People are another major resource of growth because they are a source of the grace so necessary to growth. What role has nature played in your growth, and what role is it playing now? What role have people played in your growth? What help or healing, what correction or comfort, have you received from fellow believers—and what are you receiving now? We are called to faithfully administer God's grace to one another (1 Peter 4:10). When has someone let you know that God used you in his or her life? In whose life do you think God may want to use you now? Ask him.

- **The Bible Helps People Grow:** The Bible does not stop with teaching about growth. It is actively involved in growth. As Paul wrote in 2 Timothy 3:16–17, "All Scripture is God-breathed and is useful for teaching, rebuking, correcting and training in righteousness, so that the man of God may be thoroughly equipped for every good work."

  1. *Teaching.* The Bible's teaching helps us understand the ways of God and his relationship with us. It also teaches many other realities concerning relationships, values, and the growth process. Where are you getting teaching now? Is it helping you grow? If not, where will you go to get some other teaching as well?

  2. *Rebuking.* No amount of teaching is enough to cure our tendencies to stray, rebel, be self-centered, or be in denial. So we need rebuking to confront us with our transgressions. When has the Spirit used a verse or passage of Scripture to help you recognize your sin? Be specific. When has a fellow believer graciously confronted you about a sin and used Scripture not to bash you, but to rebuke you?

  3. *Correcting.* Scripture can straighten out our errors—not necessarily errors due to sin or rebellion, but the mistakes we make out of ignorance or lack of awareness. When has God's Word spoken to you about something you hadn't understood or known about before? Be specific. What truth are you understanding more accurately as a result of your current Bible study?

  4. *Training in righteousness.* The Bible trains us to become godly, mature, and upright people. When has the Bible helped you turn from evil and do good (Ps. 34:14)? Tell of a specific struggle, either current or past. When has the Bible helped produce in you wise and sound judgment (Prov. 2:2)? In what aspect of righteousness is God training you through your current study of his Word?

5. *Comfort and strength.* As we grow spiritually, we need encouragement and support. In the same way that we receive comfort from God in prayer and from friends who listen and love us, we can be refreshed through the Scriptures. What passage(s) of Scripture do you often turn to for comfort, encouragement, or refreshment? On what particular occasion or during what season of your life has the Bible been an especially significant source of comfort and strength?

6. *Identification with fellow growers.* The faith lives of people in the past help us identify our struggles, sins, and victories (see Rom. 15:4). Whose walk of faith has been an encouragement to you the way David's story was to me?

7. *Spiritual warfare.* Jesus focused on the Scriptures when he was tempted by the Devil (Matt. 4:1–11). Also, the Word is the only offensive weapon in the listing of the armor of God (Eph. 6:11–17). When has the Spirit brought to mind a verse of Scripture just when you needed to stand strong against temptation? What passage(s) might be good to memorize and wield as a weapon against the Enemy?

Life and light are within the Bible. So when people expose themselves to the pages of the Bible, something profound happens. They come into contact with the God of the universe and with the way he sees the world and us.

THE BIBLE AND THE GOD OF THE BIBLE (Page 199)

Some people make the mistake of missing the one to whom the Bible is directing them. They become enamored of learning the depths and complexities of the Bible, and they forget that it points us toward God.

- Why might some people be more comfortable studying the Bible rather than meeting the one to whom it points?

- Before you open the Bible, do you ask the Holy Spirit to help you understand what you'll be reading? If so, what difference does that make in your reading? If not, make a bookmark or put a sticky note on the cover of your Bible to remind you to pray first! In time, praying first will become a habit.

The Bible was written to give us the path to God, life, and growth. Keep that as your goal, and ask God daily to bring life to you through its pages.

THE BIBLE AND PSYCHOLOGY (Page 200)

Do we need both the Bible and psychology to grow? This topic has been the topic of a great deal of discourse. We take the following position: *The Bible teaches everything that people need to grow.* All the principles and truths necessary for spiritual growth and for relating to God and others, maturing, and working out personal issues and problems have been provided.

- Before opening the *How People Grow* text, where would you have come down in the Bible versus psychology debate? In what ways has your opinion changed since reading this book?

- What is especially empowering or exciting to you about what *How People Grow* has taught you about the truths of the Bible?

Psychology's sound research and theories have been very helpful in dealing with people's problems, but they actually only serve to illuminate and support the principles of growth and healing that have always been in the Bible.

BIBLICAL ILLITERACY (Page 201)

Many Christians who have found help in growing spiritually and emotionally are not well grounded in the Bible. This biblical illiteracy is a problem because the Bible is so central to God's process of growth.

- Many people have been taught Bible content, but sometimes the teaching isn't helpful and other times it's not connected to "real life." What teaching have you been exposed to? What will you do to find healing if the teaching hasn't been helpful?

- Consider your level of biblical literacy or illiteracy. Wherever you fall on the spectrum, what are you doing to continue to grow in your knowledge of God's Word?

Many people who have taken the time to study the Scriptures have found that this simple endeavor can help them make authentic and heart-based changes within their lives forever. They are permanently and "thoroughly equipped for every good work" (2 Tim. 3:17).

PRACTICALITIES (Page 202)

You can expose yourself to the Bible in several ways, and each has its unique benefits.

- ***Listening:*** What Bible teacher(s) do you listen to regularly? Whom can you ask for recommendations about good preaching and teaching tapes or broadcasts?

- ***Reading:*** We suggest that you make a plan to read the Bible every day for the rest of your life. What resource will you use? Who will hold you accountable?

- **Quiet Time:** What have your quiet times looked like in the past? What has been most nourishing for you? What changes might enrich what you're doing now?

- **Study:** What regular program of Bible study are you involved in either through your church, with a group of fellow believers, or on your own? What opportunities are available to you?

- **Meditation:** Describe the rewards of meditating on a passage of Scripture. If this practice is new to you, try meditating—reading a passage several times, praying over it, asking God to show you himself—on one of these: Psalm 1; 15; 103; 119; John 1:14; Ephesians 4:15–16.

- **Memorization:** What Scripture passages have you hidden in your heart (Ps. 119:11)? You might memorize the following: Micah 6:8; Matthew 5:6; Romans 8:1; 1 Corinthians 10:13; Galatians 6:1; Ephesians 4:31–32; and 1 John 1:9.

- **Formal Study:** What seminary, Bible school, or church classes—either on campus or online—might be interesting?

As you expose yourself to the Bible, experiment with different methods and preferences. See what suits your style and reaps the most benefits. And take note of whether you find that your heart, life, and relationships are being connected to God and his love for you.

RESTAURANT REVISITED (Page 204)

Remember Cindy, my restaurant friend? I would respond differently to her question today.

* How did my new answer to Cindy's question (page 205 of the text) compare with your attempt at the beginning of this workbook chapter to answer her?

* What does my answer suggest to you about the power and relevance of God's Word?

The Bible points us to the life of God in so many ways. Delve deeply into its life-giving truths and stories. And find in the chapters that follow many essential elements of growth about which the Bible teaches us.

Lord God, you are my Creator. You are the source of all growth. Thank you for the work you are doing in me—and the work you want to do in me. I ask that you would teach me to cooperate with you. And thank you for your powerful Word that points me to you. May I become a better student of your Word so that I may know you better and so that you may grow me into the person you want me to be. I pray in Jesus' name. Amen.

TIPS FOR GROWERS:

* Explore how you have related to the Bible: Have you seen it as being about religion and not the rest of life? Have you experienced it as a book of prohibitions to deprive you of fun? Or have you seen the Bible as bringing life and light to your soul?

* Begin studying the scope and nature of the Bible—its uniqueness and power in people's lives over the course of several millennia—to understand how it is a resource for your everyday life.

- Whenever you open the Bible, first ask God to reveal himself to you through the Scriptures.

- The teaching "All you need is the Bible" is an unbiblical concept. Understand that the Bible teaches that, more than just reading its words, we need to live its truths.

CHAPTER ELEVEN

No Pain, No Gain: The Role of Suffering and Grief

Physical exercise and suffering is analogous to personal growth and suffering. Pain can bring health. The same God who designed and created our muscles designed and created our souls. Just as we stretch our muscles to make them stronger, God stretches our souls to grow them into something stronger and better.

• What is your attitude toward exercise?

• Pain in our souls can bring growth and health. Certain suffering tears down aspects of our character that need to be torn down and builds up new aspects that we need to live as we were designed to live.

— Describe a season of suffering from your own life. What character growth resulted from it?

— Suffering can take us to places where one more season of "comfort" cannot. What came out of the season of suffering you just described that would not have come out of a season of comfort?

• Suffering can be good, but suffering can also be terrible. Such suffering inflicts evil on a person's heart and soul and is totally outside God's desire. Although God can bring good out of the experience, the experience itself is no good at all.

— What suffering has inflicted evil on your heart and soul?

— What good has God brought out of that experience?

• Remember the mugging and the surgery? There is therapeutic suffering, and there is destructive suffering at the hands of evil people. The key is to be able to tell the difference between the two and to apply the right kind of experience to each.

— When you were "mugged," did anyone tell you that God was trying to teach you a lesson or that what had happened was a result of your sin? How helpful was such feedback? How did it make you feel?

We are to "bear one another's burdens" (Gal. 6:2 NASB) and help one another through tough times. We hurt, and we need help.

GOOD PAIN (Page 208)

As we just said, some pain is "good for nothing" and should not be treated as if it has value. But other suffering does produce growth. We call this "good pain."

- Dan's story (pages 209–13 of the text) illustrates how good pain can lead to growth.
  — At what points could you relate to Dan? When have your old coping methods no longer worked?

  — What did you learn from what I said to Dan?

  — What was good about Dan's pain?

- Dan was a sick, incomplete man in need of major surgery. And that is what God did in his life. The circumstances were the "wounding" from the surgeon's knife; the deep work in the soul was the constructive surgery itself. In the end, Dan was put back together much better than before.
  — What hurts from the past have circumstances in your life forced you to face? Or what hurts are current circumstances forcing you to face?

  — What kind of "deep work in the soul" have you benefited from or might you benefit from?

The old Dan died. God himself put him to death. But whenever God crucifies one of his children, he resurrects him or her to glory.

STRETCHING THE SOUL AND PUSHING THROUGH
(Page 213)

We all have coping mechanisms that cover up pain, help us deal with fear, cope with relational inabilities, and help us hold it all together. Trials and suffering push those mechanisms past the breaking point so we find out where we need to grow. Then true spiritual growth begins at deeper levels, and we are healed. Righteousness and character take the place of coping.

- The kind of suffering that breaks down and stretches the "weak muscle" of the soul and replaces it with stronger muscle is good. In this suffering, the prize we win is character (Rom. 5:3–5).

— In character growth, we stretch to grow. We push through the fear, the vulnerability, and the pain. Which of the following painful and scary things (and the list goes on and on!) have you pushed through?

Reaching out from a vulnerable heart

Making a vulnerable heart available to be known

Confessing sin and failure to yourself and others

Facing hurt and pain and allowing others to see it and be there in it

Taking risks in new areas of performance

Taking risks to be more honest

Taking risks in relational confrontation

Dealing with trauma and pain from the past

Becoming assertive

Becoming active in life to get your needs met

Taking responsibility for your weaknesses and growing beyond them

Learning to grieve

Learning to forgive

Learning to ask for forgiveness and to make amends

Learning to reconcile difficult relationships

— Which of the items listed above is a "weak muscle" for you? Is God going to let those muscles stay weak? Why or why not?

- God requires a lot from us. In fact, he requires it all. Maturity and completion are our goals. He does say that we will not get there completely, but at the same time he tells us to press on toward those goals at all times (Phil. 3:12; Eph. 5:13–16).

  — Suffering is the path to righteousness Jesus modeled for us, and he modeled how to do it right. He went through it all without sin and with obedience (Heb. 5:7– 9). What sins characterized your attitudes, words, and actions in your last season of suffering? What temptations to disobey did you encounter?

  — Jesus modeled going through suffering with an eye toward his Father, knowing that he could deliver him if he desired, but that God had a greater purpose in having him go through the process instead. What can you do to keep an eye toward your heavenly Father in your current (or next) season of suffering?

As you work through things in your own life, value the suffering that builds character. Look at your trials with the question, "What can I learn through this?" And ask God for wisdom to find out what steps of maturity and growth have to happen in your life. If you take these steps, you will not have to walk the same path again.

BAD PAIN (Page 215)

Bad pain comes from repeating old patterns and avoiding the suffering it would take to change them; many times people suffer because of their own character faults.

- People can come alongside but not tell sufferers that their suffering is the fruit of their own character and is of no value unless they see it as a wake-up call.

— When have people offered you comfort or a spiritual pep talk about how God is with you in your testing instead of helping you see what weak character muscles contributed to the suffering? What was the result of their "help"? Did you, for example, take on a false martyr role?

— When have you offered someone comfort or a spiritual pep talk about how God is with that person in the testing instead of helping him or her see what weak character muscles contributed to the suffering? Why did you do that?

- Bad pain is basically *wasted* pain. It is the pain we go through to avoid the good pain of growth that comes from pushing through. It is the wasted pain we encounter as we try to avoid grief and true hurt that needs to be worked through. It is the wasted pain of trying to get a person to love us or approve of us instead of facing the loss and moving on.

  — Which of these examples of bad pain have you experienced or are you currently experiencing? Why did you choose/are you choosing the bad pain instead of the good pain possible in that situation?

  — Here are other examples of bad pain (described in greater detail on page 216 of the text):

  Pain that comes from avoiding pain

  Pain that comes from not facing a character pattern that needs to be changed

  Pain that comes from picking the wrong kinds of people to be close to in friendship or romance

  Pain that comes from repeating failing patterns in work and performance

  Pain that comes from addictions

  Pain that comes from avoiding growth

  Pain that comes from not separating from destructive family of origin patterns

Pain that comes from lack of forgiveness and not letting go of bad relationships and injuries

Pain that comes from desiring things from the past that will never come true

Pain that comes from isolation and not learning how to become interdependent

Which of these examples of bad pain have you experienced or perhaps are experiencing now? What could you have done (or can you do) to turn the situation into one of good pain?

Much pain comes from not facing our own issues that repetitively cause pain. Not facing the growth that we have to face always leads to further suffering—and the further suffering gets progressively worse. If a person is not facing things, the dynamics and symptoms and relationships get worse as time goes on.

HOW TO AVOID BAD PAIN AND EMBRACE GOOD PAIN (Page 217)

Here are three important points.

- *First, do not refer to pain and suffering caused by character patterns as "growth pain."* This is not legitimate suffering. This is the fruit of a lack of growth.

  — What pain and suffering have you experienced because of a certain character pattern? Be brutally honest with yourself as you look at your life. You might even ask someone who knows you well to help you look for patterns in your life.

  — The Bible tells us that if we do not confront people to take ownership of their problems, we share in the guilt of those problems (Ezek. 3:18–21; Lev. 19:17). Whom could you have confronted in the past? Whom could you confront now, speaking the truth in love and enabling that person to grow rather than repeat a mistake?

- *Second, own worthless pain so that it can be redeemed and turned into "good pain."* If you can see the character patterns causing your pain, you can redeem and change them. If you can own a pattern, you can change that pattern.

  — What character pattern do you need to own?

  — What might the genuine desire to change require of you?

- *Third, convert worthless suffering into redemptive suffering.* Realize that you are not just a victim like the man in the story of the Good Samaritan (Luke 10:27–37).

  — Why is the victim role a popular one these days?

  — When have you cast yourself as a victim? Why did you make—or are you making—that choice? What is a healthier option?

It is a very human trait to try to avoid the suffering of discipline and growth. We all do it. But the wiser we become, the more we value the pain of growth and despise the avoidance patterns in our lives.

PETER: THE RELUCTANT SUFFERER (Page 218)

The Bible says that having an attitude of embracing suffering will protect us against sin (1 Peter 4:1–2). The apostle Peter illustrates this point, as does Dan's story.

- Right in the midst of Peter's attempt to get Jesus to avoid the suffering he came to do—the suffering he came to model for us as the path to resurrection—Jesus calls us not to avoid suffering, but to embrace it (Matt. 16:24–25).

— What had Dan done to try to "save himself"?

— What happened as a result of him picking up his cross, of embracing the suffering and dying to his old ways?

- Consider how similar your current situation (or a past situation) is to Dan's circumstances.

— What are you doing (or have you done) to try to "save yourself"?

— What has finally compelled you to pick up your cross, to embrace the suffering and die to your old ways?

— What sin has embracing your suffering helped you avoid?

As Dan faced his cross and went through the death experience of things he had lost and the character patterns that needed to die, he found life as he had never known it before. By suffering, by picking up his cross and being obedient to the suffering of growth and character change, he experienced salvation from his sin.

THE REAL SUFFERING OF CHRIST (Page 221)

Most likely we will not face a brutal execution as Jesus did. So how are we to identify with the sufferings of Christ? How can we arm ourselves with his attitude and purpose? Here are a few ways, ones that are intimately connected to the growth process.

- ***The Kenosis, or Emptying Experience of Godhood:*** The first way to arm ourselves with the attitude of Christ is to "empty" ourselves. It is a humbling, suffering, lifelong experience to empty ourselves of the wish to be godlike. It is impossible for us to play God, yet we try. To humble ourselves constantly and to take the role of God's bondservant is the path of all growth.

  — In what situations or roles are you tempted to play God?

  — Describe one or two humbling moments in your life. What growth came (or could have come) out of them?

  — Circumstances can humble us, but what can you do to humble yourself, to choose the path of humility as Jesus did? Be specific.

Life only works when we are being human. It does not work when we are playing God.

- ***"Not My Will, But Yours Be Done":*** The second way to arm ourselves with the attitude of Christ is to submit to God's will. In Gethsemane, Jesus submitted to the path God had placed before him. This submission to suffering was the key. In all growth, we have to bend the knee to God's path for us rather than going our own way.

  — The most basic means of choosing our own way and not God's is to decide not to suffer. When have you chosen your way by taking Satan's solution and giving in to the temptation to medicate pain (with sex, substances, performance, or materialism, for instance) instead of dealing with it? What were the consequences? In what ways are you currently choosing not to suffer?

— A more subtle way we choose our own way and not God's is to rely on our old defense maneuvers. To choose God's will and not our own is to face our defense mechanisms and give them up. When we do so, we find that we have to deal with our problems. What are some of your favorite defense maneuvers? (If you're not sure, ask someone close to you who will be honest.) What is God's will for you in those situations when your defenses arise? Which defense maneuver are you relying on right now?

Like Tony, you can learn to do what Jesus did in tough situations: "the will of God."

- *Not Returning Evil for Evil:* The third way to arm ourselves with the attitude of Christ is to not retaliate. Tony discovered the dynamic of not "returning evil for evil" when he realized that his level of health and maturity could not be dependent on someone else's. If it were, he would be a slave to someone else's immaturity.

  — Describe a time when you were "a slave to someone else's immaturity," when you were drawn into sick patterns or sick relatedness by someone else's sick patterns. What would you do in that situation now? If you are currently in such a situation, what will you do to remove yourself from that slavery?

  — Ultimately, we are only as healthy as our ability to relate as God relates. He is honest, loving, and forgiving, and he communicates well, is able to be vulnerable, and so on. So how healthy are you? Which of these traits are stronger than others? Which one or two could use some strengthening right away? What will you do to strengthen those traits?

— Jesus suffered through the dysfunction of others and did not allow it to turn him into one of them. We need to do the same as we follow his example of suffering (1 Peter 2:19–23). Whose dysfunction do you have the opportunity to suffer through? What can you learn from this suffering? (You might also consider who has the opportunity these days to suffer through your dysfunction!)

Jesus was concerned with doing the right thing, no matter what was done to him. If we would identify with that suffering, we would get well and grow much faster. We would transcend the immaturity around us and grow in spite of what is thrown at us.

- **_Picking Up the Cross:_** We have to identify with the cross of Christ. We have to be obedient to the suffering that will bring about holiness. We have to give up our own defensive and offensive attempts to save ourselves.

   — Identifying with Jesus' suffering has meant many things to believers over the years. List three or four specific examples from the lives of people you know or know about.

   — What kind of suffering or persecution has being a follower of Christ meant to you? What current suffering is due to your faith?

The internal suffering of character growth is a constant for everyone who tries to live life Jesus' way. It means that we humble ourselves and give up playing God. It means we are able to say "not my will, but yours." And it means we will not return evil for evil, but overcome evil with good (Rom. 12:21). All of these responses are a very real part of how people grow.

GRIEF: GOD'S CURE FOR WHAT ISN'T RIGHT (Page 227)

Grief is the toughest pain we have to deal with. It is not the worst human experience, because it leads to resolution, but it is the most difficult for us to enter into voluntarily, which is the only way to get into it.

- *The Loss Itself—Reality:* For grief to occur, something bad has to happen. What opportunities for grief have you experienced? What opportunity are you perhaps experiencing now?

- *Protest—I Don't Want This to Be True:* When something bad occurs, we protest the reality. One way we protest is by becoming numb or denying what is happening. Another way we protest is by screaming, "No! This cannot be happening!" Then we usually try to change reality. Our protest turns into bargaining.

  — What form(s) has your protest against reality taken?

  — What bargains have you attempted, especially when dealing with less tangible losses? With whom, for instance, have you been trying to live out the bargain that if you were prettier, thinner, smarter, a higher achiever, the love would be there?

  — What are you doing now to protest against a current reality? And what bargain are you attempting to make as you deal with a loss?

- *Despair or Depression—The Giving In:* When our protests and bargaining do not work, we realize that what has happened is really true. This is the beginning of grief proper; it is an embracing of the loss. We become aware that this reality is not going to change.

— Why is this step so difficult?

— Why is this step so important?

— What has kept you—or is keeping you—from facing the real despair that you carry inside?

— What will you do to go about embracing the loss that is behind that despair? Be specific. When will you take the first step?

- **Sadness, Loss, and Grief Proper—Letting Go and Saying Good-bye:** When we realize the truth and hit bottom, we "lose it." We break and we cry. This sadness is the letting go of the reality and saying good-bye to what can never be. But it is the beginning of true healing as well (see Solomon's words in Ecclesiastes 7:3).

— To what do you need to say, "I will never have it, so I will let go of the wish"?

— What do you find helpful about the image of your wish being like a leaf falling into a stream, free of the tree that lost it, and going away?

- ***Resolution and Resurrection—Understanding and Becoming Available:*** The sadness goes away. And, as Solomon said, then the heart is happy. It is happy because it is now available for new things: new desires, new attachments, new hope, new energy, and everything that springtime brings.

  — What newness have you seen someone take away from an experience of loss and grief?

  — What newness have you yourself experienced after a season of loss and grief?

Whether good or bad, what was lost was an experience, and from it we take understanding and wisdom for the rest of life. The death experience has given away to the resurrection of a new life.

- ***If Grief Is So Good for Us, Why Don't We Grieve?*** If grieving is the answer to so many of life's problems, why don't we just do it?

  — First, we usually hold funerals only when someone dies, but we also need to grieve other things. The problem is that we don't often see those experiences as losses. For which of your life experiences would a funeral have been appropriate? Which life experiences would you be freer of and benefiting from if you acknowledged the significant loss involved? For what current or very recent life experience would a funeral be appropriate? When will you have the funeral?

  — Another important reason people cannot grieve the way they need to is that they lack resources. If there is not enough love to sustain us, we cannot let go of anything, even something bad. Where might you go to find love to support you so that you can let go of something? To what structured experience like a group, a therapist, or a prayer partner will you commit to deal with your grief and receive the support you need?

We need love, support, and comfort for grieving. We also need structure. We need time and space and structured activities for grieving. Furthermore, the Bible recognizes that grief is only done in community. Being heard, empathized with, understood, and supported gives us the life support we need to go through the surgery of grief.

The psalmist was right when he said, "Weeping may remain for a night, but rejoicing comes in the morning" (Ps. 30:5). The Bible affirms it and commands it, and science proves it to be true. There really is such a thing as "good grief."

Lord God, as I think about grief, I find hope and comfort in your sovereignty. With you in control, I shouldn't be surprised that good pain brings growth. Reveal to me any good-for-nothing pain in my life. Reveal to me the character patterns that are causing me to suffer. Lord, the next time I have an opportunity to grieve, may I walk through the process in a healthy way as Jesus did and with people who can give me the love I need. And I know you'll be walking through it with me too. I pray in Jesus' name. Amen.

TIPS FOR GROWERS:

- Define "muggings" and "the suffering of growth." Determine whether you have been blamed for the muggings of life and note when you have not seen the growth value of "good pain." Work on adopting as your own Peter's attitude that suffering is armor.

- Review the list on pages 213–14 of the text. Which of these painful and scary things would you do well to tackle?

- Look in the mirror:

  — Determine what bad or worthless pain in your life you need to see differently. Convert it to helpful suffering. Take a look at the issues you would do well to embrace.

  — Make sure that you are not seeking consolation for things you need to change.

  — Look for repetitive patterns in your life that you should own up to.

  — See whether any aspects of the suffering of Christ are present in your life:
  Kenosis
  Not my will
  Facing pain and stopping medicating or using defenses
  Not returning evil for evil

  — Take an inventory of the grief you need to face. Get the support you need and go through it.

CHAPTER TWELVE

Growing Tasty Fruit: Becoming a Righteous Person

When I (Henry) hit bottom, Matthew 6:33 turned my life around. This verse invited me to believe that God could help me put my life together. Somehow I skipped over the "his righteousness" part of the verse.

- I soon found out that seeking God's righteousness meant that I would find a legal righteousness—forgiveness before God—through *faith*, not through *works*. God accepted me on the basis of what Jesus did, and I was declared "righteous" by him (Rom. 10:4). What I did not immediately discover, though, was that I would also have to work on living out in my soul and in my life the righteousness I had in the sight of God.

  — What changes do you need to make in your personality and character to be more like God, more "righteous"? What steps can you take to make those changes? Who will help you by praying and holding you accountable?

  — What (unrighteous) dynamics and patterns in your life are contributing to your problems? What will you do to get free of those dynamics and patterns? Again, who will help?

— Look back over your life, especially at seasons of growth. What has been "given to you" as you've sought God's kingdom and righteousness?

• Some of the things we want from God are fruits of our becoming more mature and righteous as we work with him. And God often only gives us things we are mature enough to use. So until we grow, we will not have them.

— When God put me through a process of growth, I saw, first, that I carried around some unresolved pain and, second, that, while I was very relational and social, I really did not let people get close to me. What has God shown you about yourself since you started reading *How People Grow*?

— Changing meant turning from doing things my way to doing things God's way. What things in your life are you still doing your way rather than God's way?

Three characteristics of people who do things God's way are, simply put, repentance (Eph. 4:22–24), understanding and insight (Phil. 1:9–10), and discipline (Heb. 12:11). Let's take a look at each of these three in greater detail.

TURNING FROM WORLDLY WAYS TO KINGDOM WAYS (Page 238)

The first characteristic of a person who does things God's way is *repentance*. To have the life we desire, we have to live according to God's ways.

• It is truly amazing to see what happens in people's lives when they shift from seeing the right way as something they "should" do to seeing it as the only way they will have life. Any of us motivated to grow must see doing things the "right" way as the only way life is going to work. God gives us his laws so that our lives will work well and we will prosper.

— When has one of God's "shoulds" prompted rebellion in you? Give a specific example.

— Redefine that "should" in terms that remind you that it is a marker on the path to life. (You'll find some examples in the list on pages 239–40).

• To grow and find life worth living, you must seek the ways of God (how his kingdom operates), and you must live and internalize these ways for yourself. To *find* his ways is to find the kingdom; to *live* his ways is to find righteousness. The kingdom of God, which seeks weakness, brokenness, righteousness, and purity of heart, is altogether different from the kingdom of this world, which seeks power and victory.

— Review Jesus' teaching in the Sermon on the Mount (listed on pages 242–43 of the text). What is your overall reaction to the list? Is it, for instance, encouraging in tone?

— Which two or three statements are especially meaningful for you today? What will you do in response to each? Be specific.

Jesus did not teach about "religion," but about a healthy life: reality. This is one of the messages of this book: *Getting righteous and aligned with the ways of the kingdom and getting healthy are one and the same thing.*

UNDERSTAND AND GAIN INSIGHT (Page 243)

The second characteristic of people who do things God's way is that they seek understanding and insight. We must find out what is best and gain insight into our lives to apply it.

- We should always be learning the ways of the kingdom and all the things God tells us to do. We need to be taught the principles of relationships, healing, and life. What are you doing to learn what God wants you to do? List your involvement with teaching, Bible studies, growth groups, books and tapes, and seminars.

- Knowledge is important, but it is not enough. We also need to know how to apply that knowledge to our own lives so that we can develop the purity that will lead to the fruit of righteousness. What are you doing to gain in-depth insight into your life? List your involvement with work, feedback, correction, digging inside your heart and soul, and prayer, specifically about your own character dynamics and patterns.

- Remember Patrick? He was content only to stay "strong in the Word" instead of also joining with a group of people who were looking into their "issues"—until his marriage was in trouble. In a group with some other men, Patrick learned much about himself and his interactions with people. A key for Patrick was finding out that the righteousness the Bible talks about is not just to be learned and preached, but to be realized at personal levels as well.

  — Where will you go to discover what is true about you—and when will you do so?

— Who can and will offer you feedback about how your patterns work and what you could do differently?

Small-group participants make such discoveries and receive important, often life-changing, feedback. They gain insight, and they find out how best to proceed. This is what the Bible says to do, and research shows that it works.

DISCIPLINE (Page 247)

We look for the "quick fix." We all want the "harvest of righteousness." But the clear teaching of the Bible, life, and all the research is that growth takes time. To receive the fruit we want, we must commit to discipline.

• What disciplines of growth are you committed to or would you consider committing to? Some choices are small groups, counseling, classes, a fresh look at your marriage, and a reevaluation of your everyday habits.

• All this effort takes time, and often it is painful. But what true growers learn is that the pain is temporary and the fruit is long-lasting. What evidence of this truth have you seen in someone's life or experienced in your own?

Someone once said that pain is dysfunction leaving the body. It hurts to grow past whatever weakness or sickness you had or to have it removed. But this kind of pain is good, and it will not return again. And the lessons you learn will last forever.

PUTTING IT ALL TOGETHER (Page 248)

A relationship with God is the answer to all we seek. If we seek first Jesus' kingdom and his righteousness, all the things we are looking for will be provided.

- Seeking God first means that we know him as the God of grace who is for us. We must give up our own self-help programs. Ask God to show you what those are in your life.

- God is not only a God of grace; he is also a God of truth. So getting well means that we have to discover a lot of truth and follow it. Again, ask the Lord to show you the truth about yourself.

Seeking righteousness is about learning and about becoming a person of life instead of death. In the end the "right" way is the only way.

Lord God, let me first thank you for the gift of righteousness that is mine because of your Son's death on the cross for my sin. And then let me confess how difficult it is to live out that righteousness in my soul and in my life. Show me, Lord, where I am living life my way, where I need to repent and live according to your ways. Tell me what you want me to do, and then give me the courage to act. Guide me to the discipline that will help me grow. I want to know you, God of grace and God of truth, and I want to grow in you. I pray in Jesus' name. Amen.

TIPS FOR GROWERS:

- Consider your attitude toward righteousness and see whether you resist the concept. Accept the truth that "right really is good for you"; that it is much more than just "being good." It is the way to get the life you desire. It is the way to the "good life."

- Take an inventory of the specific areas of your life that are not "righteous." See them as, at best, keeping you from what you desire and, at worst, destroying you. Repent of the lack of righteousness in these areas.

- Change your "I should" thinking about righteousness to "I need to." Getting "right" with God is not something you "should" do; it is the thing you truly "need" to do.

- Determine in what relationship(s) you can gain deeper insight and understanding about yourself and about where you fall short of righteous living. The process of sanctification is much deeper than just knowing the concepts. The concepts must interfere with where you are and call you to change.

CHAPTER THIRTEEN

The Value of Pruning: Discipline

Ayoung woman named Kara came into my (John's) office to talk. "Here's my problem," she said. "I tend to be a flake." She didn't seem to have any resistance to being organized, nor did she seem to be sabotaging herself. I suggested to Kara that she check in with her husband and some friends at certain times during the day to encourage her and share how her to-do list was going. When self-discipline is found wanting, we need other discipline from outside of us. Kara went to work, and I wasn't surprised when she called me a while later and said things were much better. She was seeing more of an ability to stay on task in her life.

WHY THE PAIN? (Page 251)

The Bible teaches that everyone needs discipline and correction to grow (Prov. 3:11). Along with all the other elements of growth we deal with in this book, discipline is a necessary—in fact, a principal—one.

- The Bible has many meanings for the word *discipline*, such as chastening, correcting, instructing, reproving, and warning. The idea for our discussion is that discipline in its broadest sense is *training to learn self-control*. Our need for discipline applies to much more than problems in organization and structure. It applies to every area of life in which we are not operating as we should, from attitudes to relationship conflicts to faith struggles.

  — What area of your life comes to mind when you read the definition "training to learn self-control"?

— If you don't have good self-discipline, you only get it from other discipline: We become disciplined by being disciplined by God and other people. We need to be disciplined to learn self-control because we are not in control of ourselves. Give recent evidence from your own life that you are not always in control of yourself.

Self-control provides a structure for love. People who have internal discipline have learned to run their lives so that God's love flows through them in very fruitful, fulfilling ways. If love is the heart of the person, discipline is the skeleton, giving a person form and protection.

• Discipline is painful, yet it assists in growing us up. It is driven not by anger or punitiveness, but by caring, "because the Lord disciplines those he loves, and he punishes everyone he accepts as a son" (Heb. 12:6).

— What negative associations do you have with the concept of discipline? What are the roots of those thoughts and images?

— With what positive associations or better understanding of discipline can you replace those thoughts and images?

• Discipline is related to suffering, though it is not the same. Suffering involves any discomfort we go through, be it as serious as the loss of a loved one or as trivial as getting a traffic ticket. However, while suffering speaks more to the *experience* of discomfort, pain, or loss, discipline is more concerned with the *goal* of growth and self-control. Explain why dieting is discipline rather than suffering.

- Submitting to discipline is difficult because we must allow something to be done to us. We are being disciplined. A certain loss of control and self-protection is necessary when we want to learn discipline.

  — Think about discipline you've experienced. Describe the loss of control and self-protection involved.

  — Although discipline is a process we receive, it does not mean we are passive in it. We are an active part in the discipline we allow to happen to us. We act, for instance, in response to what the discipline reveals to us about ourselves (our indirectness, our tendency to withdraw, or our bluntness). What are you doing in response to any discipline you're currently experiencing?

Discipline is one of the necessary ingredients of spiritual growth. Let's look more closely at what's involved.

THE INGREDIENTS OF DISCIPLINE (Page 253)

Several aspects to discipline operate in our hearts and aid our spiritual growth. Some are qualities of the person being trained, and others are qualities of the process. When the discipline works as it should, these all add up to much growth in the person.

What the Grower Must Provide —

- **Receptiveness:** We need to be receptive to discipline's training. The more we embrace the necessary pains of growth, the more discipline bears fruit (Heb. 12:11).

  — Think about your openness to discipline's training. Are you more like King David or the Pharaoh of Egypt? Support your answer with specific evidence from your life.

— One gauge of receptiveness is whether people ask for feedback on how they affect others. What does this standard suggest about your receptiveness to the sanctification that discipline can bring? Who and how often do you ask about how you affect them?

- **Confession:** To "confess" is to agree with the truth. When God or others are disciplining us, we need to agree on the issue or problem. When we confess, we are aligning ourselves with the process of growth and repair (James 5:16).

  — Why does it make sense that confession begins the process of repair?

  — Why do you struggle to confess, to agree with whatever truth is the focus of discipline?

  — What do you need to confess right now? What issue or problem do you need to openly acknowledge as either in need of discipline or as the reason for current discipline from God or others?

- **Repentance:** When we encounter God's discipline, we need to be willing not only to agree with the truth, but to turn around or repent. Repentance means that we truly will change what needs to be changed.

  — Why do so many of us stop before repentance at the step of confession?

— Describe an act or process of repentance from your own life. What did God do to let you know you needed to change your ways? What steps did you take to make that change? Who supported you and what kind of support did they offer? If you can't think of an illustration from your own life, consider what that means.

— What do you need to repent of now? What kind of support do you need? To whom will you turn for that support? When will you begin?

What the Process Must Provide —

- **A Source:** Discipline must come from the outside until we develop self-control and maturity. God provides more than one source of discipline.

  — First, God chastens and corrects us directly. Give an example from your own life. What was the issue and how did God communicate to you?

  — Second, people are a source of discipline. Who in your life is — or would be — caring, honest, perceptive, and loving enough to correct you when you stray?

  — Third, reality is a source of discipline. God has constructed the universe to operate with certain laws. When we disobey those laws, we feel the pain of the consequences. When has reality or, more specifically, the painful consequences of your actions alerted you to a growth task you needed to attend to? Be specific.

- *Empathy from Others:* Discipline must be administered with gentleness and care.

  — What can people who are offering correction do to show that they care deeply about the person they're correcting?

  — What can a person do to communicate that the desire is correction, not punishment?

- *Pain:* Discipline generally requires pain to be effective. Pain signals a problem to which we should pay attention. The kinds and dosages of pain differ according to our need. A person with a receptive heart needs less pain to get the message.

  — When has significant pain been necessary for you to get a message? Be specific about both the pain and the message.

  — What evidence (if any) do you see in your life that your heart is becoming more receptive and you are needing less pain to get discipline's message? Be specific.

- *Time:* Sometimes discipline performs its work very quickly, and sometimes not so quickly, depending on the attitude of the grower, the severity of the issue, how early in life the problem began, and the spiritual and emotional resources available to the grower.

  — Think of an example from your own life (or the life of someone you know) that illustrates either the speed or slowness of growth. In that situation, which of the following was—or wasn't—a factor?

The attitude of the grower
The severity of the issue being dealt with
How early in life the problem began
The spiritual and emotional resources available to help

— What kind of spiritual and emotional resources can you draw from? Be specific and note how each can help issues be resolved quickly.

— What is going on in your life right now that reminds you that you need to be patient with the process and give the discipline more time?

• **Internalization:** Internalization is the process of emotional learning that means a person has made the experience a part of herself. She has taken in the lesson and grown from it.
  — What healthier attitudes or behaviors have you internalized through the years? Give a specific example or two, noting the positive experiences that contributed to your learning the lesson.

  — What is one healthier attitude or behavior you would like to be able to internalize? What are some possible steps toward that goal? Where will you go for support?

WHAT NEEDS DISCIPLINING? (Page 258)

How do we know what to correct and what to let go? Here are some guidelines for how to think about disciplining.

- *Problems Arising from Ignorance:* Some people are ignorant of the issues. They simply don't know they are a problem.

  — Does this description fit someone you know? If the problem is worth confronting, what might you say to speak the truth in love?

  — When has someone confronted you about some aspect of how you act that you didn't even recognize as a problem?

  — To whom can you go to ask if you are ignorant and unaware of problem areas in your own life?

- *Problems in Lack of Structure:* The structure of discipline can help people who struggle to confront problems with others stay focused on goals, make good choices, and think long-term.

  — When have you seen clearly defined parameters and consequences (elements of discipline) provide someone with the structure necessary to grow? Explain.

  — What issue in your life might you be able to overcome with appropriately structured discipline? Where will you go to find that discipline?

- *Character Patterns:* We need to be aware of, and discipline, disruptive character patterns.

— Patterns of emotional detachment, passivity, devaluing love, controlling others, irresponsibility, self-centeredness, and perfectionism can cause such external problems as depression, anxiety, marital and dating struggles, financial struggles, and substance abuse. What insight does this question give you into someone's behavior?

— What insight into your own behavior and character does this list offer you? As we asked before, where can you go to find discipline that could be helpful?

- *Erring toward Comfort:* Be aware that some spiritual growth concerns may need more love than correction.

  — Who in your life might need love more than he/she needs correction? What is keeping you from sharing God's love with that person?

  — What issue in your life do you think calls more for love than correction? You might ask a pastor or trusted friend for another perspective.

DISCIPLINE BUSTERS (Page 260)

Sadly, we all tend to sabotage the growth process. Here are four of the ways we can turn from God.

- *Denial:* Denial is not admitting the truth about a problem. One kind of denial is when we keep something hurtful away from our awareness; the other is when we don't want to admit we have responsibility for something, such as how selfish we can be.

— Why do you think God allows the first kind of denial? Have you or someone you know experienced this kind of denial? Describe the situation—the hurt, what brought the injury into the light, and the healing that is in process.

— When have you encountered someone in denial about a current and very real problem? In what ways did that denial impact the person's relationships?

— What behavior and/or attitude might you be in denial about? If you really want to know, someone close to you might be able to help you answer this question.

• **Rationalization:** When we rationalize, we make excuses for our problem to avoid being blamed. We may admit the problem exists, but it is not our responsibility.

— How do you respond to people who make excuses and avoid taking responsibility for their behavior?

— When have you made excuses for a problem to avoid either blame or hard work? What were the consequences of your rationalization? Share how it helped the situation or made it worse.

— For what problem are you currently failing to take responsibility? Why? What is the first step to taking responsibility?

- **Minimization:** To minimize is to lessen the perception of the problem, or dilute it. A person might say, "I really don't criticize you like you think I do. You're being oversensitive."

  — When have you been on the receiving end of someone's minimization of a problem that affected you? How did you feel about that?

  — In what way—either by your attitude, action, or words—are you minimizing the effect of your behavior on another person? Why are you doing so?

- **Blame:** Blame takes the responsibility squarely off the shoulders of one and lays it on another.

  — Describe your reaction to a time when the responsible party avoided responsibility and blamed you. Why do you think the person did that?

  — Whom are you blaming for certain aspects of your life? Why are you doing so? When will you stop—and what will stopping the blame call for you to do?

At the heart of all of these "discipline busters" is our attempt to remove a bad aspect of ourselves from us. This is called "projection" (Matt. 7:1–5). People project so that they will not have to experience the discomfort of their own weaknesses and sins. These projections divide people and disrupt the growth process, so we must directly confront denial, rationalization, minimization, or blame when we become aware of it.

CASE IN POINT (Page 262)

Making oneself accountable to others can be an effective means of discipline, as shown in the personal illustration on page 262.

- What did you learn from my example of discipline bearing the fruit of writing deadlines being met?

- To what current situation in your life can you apply this approach? Be specific.

CONCLUSION (Page 263)

God disciplines those he loves. And if we stay in the correction process "correctly," we will grow in love, faith, and responsibility.

- Summarize your understanding of what it means to "stay in the correction process 'correctly.'"

- What correction process are you in the midst of? Why is the truth that God disciplines those he loves especially significant to you right now?

Discipline provides a structure for growth. Another important element that helps make us open to growth and discipline is spiritual poverty. Find out about its benefits in the next chapter.

Lord God, thank you that you discipline those you love, and that you do so with our growth and increased self-control as your goal. You know even better than I do the areas of my life where I need to exercise greater self-control. Please help me first to be open to seeing those areas where I have problems, and then help me to be open to letting your discipline do its work in me. Give me the strength to bear up under the pain and the patience to rest in your timing. Keep me focused on removing the plank in my own eye rather than being overly concerned about the speck in my brother's eye. I pray in Jesus' name. Amen.

TIPS FOR GROWERS:

- Take an inventory of how your lack of self-control has affected you spiritually, relationally, financially, or sexually; in your parenting, your career, your home maintenance, or your diet.

- Investigate why you have lacked discipline in those areas. Was the reason a lack of accountability, overharsh discipline, or your resistance to limitations? Look at any tendencies to deny, rationalize, minimize, or blame your self-control struggles. Own the problems.

- Understand that discipline can't come from willpower and commitment, as those are on the inside. When we lack self-control, we must find discipline from other-control—that is, from external structures that help us internalize discipline. Make a plan to find discipline in the context of supportive, loving relationships that will foster growth.

- See God as caring and loving, not punitive, when he disciplines you.

CHAPTER FOURTEEN

Water from a Deeper Well: Spiritual Poverty

By our very nature, we are a broken people (Rom. 7:15–24), with no hope except for God. Not everyone is aware of his or her neediness, but listen to what Jesus said of those who are: "Blessed are the poor in spirit, for theirs is the kingdom of heaven" (Matt. 5:3). The kingdom of heaven belongs to those who experience their dependency on God, like a cringing beggar absolutely dependent on others for survival.

- When have you been most aware of your neediness? Give an example or two, being specific about the contributing circumstances.

- Spiritual poverty is about living in reality. It is about experiencing our state of incompleteness before God.
  —Which of the following is contributing to any sense of incompleteness you're currently experiencing?

  Weaknesses

  Unfulfilled needs

  Emotional injuries and hurts at the hands of others

  Your own immaturities and sins

  Those parts of yourself that are not what they should be—and that you are

  Unable to repair in your own strength

—Why is spiritual poverty the cure for, among other things, narcissism and self-righteousness? What benefits have you known as a result of spiritual poverty?

- Jesus calls spiritual poverty a "blessed" condition because it helps us get closer to God. Our state of incompleteness drives us outside of ourselves to God as the source of healing and hope. When we are comfortably independent, it is easy to avoid our need for God.

    — What has God allowed to happen to you during a "comfortably independent" stage of your life to remind you of your spiritual poverty?

    — When, for instance (if at all), has God used your brokenheartedness—the state of being wounded by some loss, person, hurt, injustice, or circumstance—to bring about in you a sense of your spiritual poverty? What about that season in your life supports the truth that "the Lord is close to the brokenhearted" (Ps. 34:18)?

    — If you're currently in a season of spiritual poverty, what blessings are you aware of, if not consistently, at least from time to time?

Just about everyone would agree that we all need to grow spiritually, but we need to get to a needy place before growth can happen.

WHY SPIRITUAL POVERTY IS IMPORTANT IN HELPING PEOPLE GROW (Page 266)

Many people want to deepen their walk, become more Christlike, and know God more intimately. But they feel disconnected from those with life problems.

- Those without struggles may feel compassion and concern, but they can't relate to the struggling people they know. What problem in your life has enabled or is enabling you to relate to struggling people?

- We are not saying that everyone with life problems is poor in spirit, but those people with life problems have more opportunities to recognize their need for God's healing. What current circumstances are reminding you of your need for the Lord and his healing grace?

- We are also not saying that those who don't experience problems are in denial. Instead, they—like the friend I saw after many years had gone by—may lack a sense of their own brokenheartedness. My friend became aware of his spiritual poverty, his particular hurt and emptiness, and his brokenness, and this awareness changed his entire spiritual life.

  — What encouragement do you find in this account? What invitation? And/or what hope?

  — What action step does my friend's experience suggest to you?

My friend offers a powerful example of how spiritual poverty can help people grow. His poverty came with his insight into his family background, his acknowledgment that he grew up cut off from his feelings and tied to his work and ministry, and his new awareness that he tended to criticize others unfairly. He went to work to get emotionally connected and to give up criticism and judgment, and he became more approachable, more relational, and more open.

THE RICHNESS THAT SPIRITUAL POVERTY BRINGS
(Page 268)

Spiritual poverty—being aware of our incompleteness—orients us toward God and his ways, where he awaits us with all we need to grow and repair. Spiritual poverty is a rich part of the spiritual growth process.

- *Spiritual Poverty Is Required for a Saving Faith:* No one can become a Christian who does not admit her lostness and inability to free herself from the prison and penalty of sin (Rom. 3:23).

  — Have you acknowledged your sin and your need for a Savior and then accepted Jesus Christ as your Savior? If so, what brought you to the point of being able to admit your lostness? If not, what is keeping you from seeing that you need a Savior?

  — In what ways have you, who accepted Christ as Savior because of your brokenness, nevertheless lived your Christian life as if you were whole?

  — What unfinished parts of you do you know need to become mature and sanctified (see Col. 2:6)? What action step will you take toward that goal of maturity and sanctification? Who will support your efforts and hold you accountable?

- *Spiritual Poverty Develops a Hunger for God:* Spiritual poverty drives us to find solutions for our neediness and, ultimately, to find God. Those who know they are truly needy are more motivated to look beyond themselves to the Lord.

  — Think about the more difficult times of your life. Were those also the times you sought the Lord more passionately and/or frequently?

— Poverty drives hunger. You can't stop a needy person from grasping onto God, while many people in less severe circumstances easily fall away. The more broken we are, the more God can grow us up. Where have you seen this pattern in your own life?

— What does this discussion make you want to do about the brokenness that you don't want to look at, are trying to deny, or are blaming on someone else? When will you take a step and look at the brokenness, acknowledge it, and/or accept responsibility for dealing with it?

- *Spiritual Poverty Helps Us Endure the Pain of Growth:* Spiritual growth is hard work. It requires sacrifice, suffering, loss, and commitment. It means losing your life to find your life in Christ (Matt. 16:25). Ultimately, the pain of growth is more bearable than the pain of our poverty.

   — When have you sensed for yourself that the pain of growth is more bearable than the pain of spiritual poverty?

   — Spiritual poverty makes it hard to go backward in the growth process. Once your eyes are opened to your need, it is difficult to live as though you had none. What about yourself and your neediness are your eyes open to now that you haven't always seen? What growth is that awareness prompting?

- *Spiritual Poverty Keeps Us Living Relationally:* Spiritual poverty and brokenheartedness give us emotional connectedness, both to God and to safe people. We learn to receive comfort, support, and acceptance from others.

— Coming to the end of ourselves reduces us to a childlike state of need and helplessness, which Jesus said is good (Mark 10:15). What is helpful about the discussion of children and the way they instinctively seek out relationship?

— From whom have you received comfort, support, and acceptance as a result of your spiritual poverty? And to whom can (or did) you offer these things during their difficult times?

— If you are very much aware of your spiritual poverty right now, to whom are you turning for comfort, support, and acceptance? Or where will you go to find such people?

- ***Spiritual Poverty Helps Us Enter the Deeper Life:*** Our brokenhearted state provokes us to move beyond spiritual immaturity into a deeper walk of faith (Heb. 6:1).
    — When has your brokenheartedness resulted in a deepening of your faith in God?

    — Which of the area(s) listed below has your deeper walk taken you into?

    The mystery of God's nature

    The wonders of the Bible

    The complexities of your own character, personality, and issues

    The intricacies of intimate relationships with others

— What current brokenheartedness could be an opportunity for deepening your faith in God? What will you do to make sure that a deeper faith results? To whom will you turn? What spiritual disciplines will help?

- ***Spiritual Poverty Does Not Allow Us to Stay Shallow:*** Once we are on the path to growth, we are called to continue it at new levels (Ps. 42:7).

    — Are you disconnected, complacent, or bored with your spiritual life? Ask others if you seem that way to them.

    — If you are disconnected, complacent, or bored, will you ask God to help you become poor in spirit and thereby find him at deeper levels? Why or why not?

- ***Spiritual Poverty Guides Us to Specific Growth Areas:*** Spiritual poverty helps us find the right issues to heal. It leads us to particular areas of need and growth by making seekers out of us.

    — If spiritual poverty has made or is making you a seeker, where are you looking? What fruit has your seeking borne so far?

    — Which of the following areas of growth has your spiritual poverty helped you recognize the need to address? Or which of these topics might be an issue for you if you accepted your spiritual poverty as reality?

    Establishing a loving and worshipful relationship with God

    Maintaining deep, vulnerable relationships with others

    Being free to make decisions based on values rather than on fear or guilt

Knowing what we are and are not responsible for

Accepting our badness and weaknesses as well as those of others

Functioning as an adult rather than as a child in life and relationships

Achieving competency in some job or career area

Having a clear and balanced morality

— What steps did you take—or will you take—to address these areas of potential growth you just identified?

HOW TO DEVELOP SPIRITUAL POVERTY (Page 273)

Becoming poor in spirit is one of the most unnatural things we can do. Yet it is our only hope for spiritual growth. Actually, our task is more realizing our poverty than becoming poor. It is better to seek this quality ourselves than be forced to face it by difficult circumstances.

- **Ask God:** God will gladly show you where you are weak. He will give you the sense of incompleteness and need that keeps you close to him. Ask God to give you a sense of your spiritual poverty.

- **Become an Honest Person:** Review your life. Look for your patterns of avoiding pain, denying problems, staying away from truthful people, and trying to put a positive spin on the negative things in your life. Consider which of the following (described in greater detail on pages 274–75 of the text) are issues for you.

  Sins (selfish, rebellious behaviors and attitudes)
  Hurts and losses
  Weaknesses

- **Read the Teachings of the Bible on the Topic:** Learn what the Bible says about being poor in spirit, needy, and brokenhearted. Look at God's relationship with Israel in the Old Testament.

— What have you learned from God's Word during your hard times?

— What hope and encouragement have you found in the Bible? Be specific.

- *Get Feedback from Others:* Hungry people surround themselves with others to help them with their dependency. They get with other people to share their vulnerabilities and fill one another up.

  — What value do you think the Townsend family tradition called *character time* has? Why might some people balk at it?

  — What character growth might you be prompted to seek if you received honest feedback about the following issues? Be specific.

  Selfishness
  Withdrawing when upset and not talking about it
  Irresponsibility in household chores
  Working too much and not playing with family enough
  Chronic lateness
  Annoying someone and not stopping when that person asks for it
  Not coming when called
  Nail biting
  Getting angry too easily
  Taking kids on errands and calling it "quality time"
  Problems having regular devotional time
  Making promises and not keeping them
  Fighting instead of talking about problems

- *Seek a Wholehearted Experience of Brokenness:* Poverty of spirit requires more of us than cognitively admitting we are incomplete and needy. It affects our entire self, especially the heart. Realizing our condition before God is an overwhelmingly emotional experience, but that emotion can help us become "integrated," having our heart and head in alliance with one another. (We get our head and heart together by seeking intimate relationship with God and safe people of faith. Relationship integrates head and heart as we internalize those experiences.) Seek to understand the reality of your own brokenness with both your head and your heart.

— When have you experienced your heart and head coming together in a season of brokenness?

— Why are we to seek brokenness wholeheartedly? How will you do that?

— If you are in a season of brokenness, describe how your head understanding came about, your heart understanding, and, ideally, the integration of the two.

God reminds us, time and time again, that he likes neediness. Our life experiences might tell us to avoid need. If so, take a faith step and open up your soul to God and safe people.

Lord God, thank you for keeping me aware of my unfinished parts and therefore aware of my need for you. I know that when life is comfortable and I'm feeling capable and strong, I don't go to you as readily. May my spiritual poverty keep me hungry for you, help me endure the pain of growth, keep me in relationship with you and safe people, and enable me to enter into a deeper walk of faith. Help me to embrace wholeheartedly the gift of brokenness. I pray in Jesus' name. Amen.

TIPS FOR GROWERS:

- Realize that spiritual poverty is a blessed state and the only position from which to receive God's growth and healing. Adopt an attitude of spiritual poverty.

- Review such life experiences as loss, failure, a hungering for God, or an awareness of your incompleteness. See how God used one or more of these experiences to draw you closer to him.

- Be aware of your brokenheartedness and mindful that this is not a sinful state, but rather a state of being sinned against or simply hurt by a broken world. Accept that you are not meant to bear your brokenheartedness alone or not only with God, but also with other people.

- Confess your weakness, brokenness, and immaturity to God and some people you trust. Admit that you can't change in your own power, and acknowledge your need for outside resources to help you.

Chapter Fifteen

Following the Gardener: Obedience

O bedience sounds so simple. But even though God helps us to obey him, obedience is anything but simple.

A TALE OF THREE WIVES (Page 278)

To illustrate, look at the stories of three wives, all of whom were good-hearted Christians who loved God. Each wanted a successful marriage, and each marriage had control and communication problems that they wanted to resolve biblically and in obedience to God. But the three differed greatly on their view of obedience and how it affected their marriage problems. Consequently, the conclusions of their stories are far different from one another.

- *Jackie:* Jackie's view of obedience was devotional and external.
  — Explain what "devotional and external" obedience is. Refer to Jackie's situation if you'd like.

  — In what ways is your obedience devotional and external? Be specific in the comparisons and/or contrasts.

— What is inadequate about devotional and external obedience?

• *Kim:* Kim's view of obedience centered more on God's role in her emotions and relationships. She interpreted his ways and will as that which would lead to self-actualization.

   — Using details from Kim's story, show how she obeyed what she felt God was saying to her through her emotions and relationships.

   — In what ways is your obedience influenced by what is going on in ("what God is saying to you through") your emotions and relationships? Give a specific example.

   — Why is this reliance on emotions and relationships not a reliable way to determine the path of obedience?

• *Alison:* Alison took the best parts of the other two women's approaches to obedience. She stayed with the traditional disciplines and requirements of her faith, yet she also entered the character and relationship work the Bible teaches (Ps. 139:23–24). Her obedience runs through her entire life. And this path is bearing good fruit for her.

   — Look closely at Alison's story. What do you appreciate about her obedience? What wisdom do you see in her actions?

— What lessons from Alison's example can you apply to your own life?

— Alison's life is not based on her husband coming around, but on her orientation to God's ways and life. How does your life compare to Alison's? Cite specific details from your life.

— What about Alison's way do you resist?

These three women exemplify the approaches toward the Christian life that we see in the world. The Jackies hope that closeness to God will solve problems. The Kims grow personally and don't see how their faith is relevant. And the Alisons believe that both processes—closeness to God and personal growth—are spiritual and necessary for growth. We agree with Alison, and this chapter on obedience explores that approach.

THE NATURE OF OBEDIENCE (Page 283)

Few Christians would disagree that obedience is central to spiritual growth, but Christians often misunderstand what biblical obedience really is. One of the central meanings of "to obey" in the Bible is "to hear." When we hear God as he is, rather than as we desire him to be, we move toward true obedience.

- *A Life Direction:* A basic definition of obedience in terms of spiritual growth is "to be God-directed, not self-directed." Obedience is to look outside ourselves for our purpose, values, and decisions. After all, God designed life to be lived a certain way. When we follow his way, life works better (Deut. 6:24; Isa. 1:19–20).

  —When has your obedience led to something good? Be specific.

— Conversely, when have you lived life your way and experienced the negative consequences of your choice?

— Describe the moment you first realized the command to obey God and his ways was for your own good.

— Which of God's laws are you currently bucking? What are you experiencing as a result?

— Which of God's commands are you consciously trying to obey? What are you experiencing as a result?

- ***All of Life:*** Some people compartmentalize obedience into their religious or moral lives, but the Bible teaches and guides on all areas of life.

  — In what ways are you compartmentalizing your obedience? What aspect of your life, for instance, do you never talk to God about or seek his will for?

  — When has God spoken to your emotional, personal, and /or relational life as well as your spiritual life? What do you think he is saying to you now? Be specific.

- **All of Us:** Not only does obedience deal with all of life, but it also encompasses all of us, both inside and out. Obedience is far more profound than simply refraining from external sins. Obedience also has to do with submitting our values, emotions, and hearts to Christ's lordship (Matt. 22:37–38). This external and internal nature of obedience helps us to grow up spiritually.

  — Think again about the man who avoided intimacy (pages 284–85 of the text). His external obedience (staying in contact with people when he felt the urge to isolate) kept the tension of his feelings contained and tolerable while the internal obedience (confessing his fears of closeness and his desires to be free and distant) healed his conflicts. Choose a current issue in your life and describe both the internal and external obedience that will lead to growth.

  — Obedience also helps us deal with both the causes and the fruits of spiritual immaturity or deficit. The couple with financial struggles (page 285) needed to address simultaneously the external obedience (creating a financial plan) and the internal obedience (dealing with his spending that anesthetizes his anger and her oversaving to feel in control of herself). Addressing perhaps the same issue you just considered, explain how your obedience will help you deal with the cause of that issue as well as its fruit in your life.

  — The matter of internal and external obedience may be easier to see and understand if you're considering someone else's situation. Give an example from another person's life that illustrates the importance of both internal and external obedience as well as the way obedience makes a difference to both the cause and the fruit of that spiritual immaturity or deficit.

- **Tasks Change as Maturity Increases:** We are all called to follow God in the basic requirements of life: loving God and others (Matt. 22:36–40); seeking God

(Amos 5:4); being just, kind, and humbly walking with God (Micah 6:8); and living by faith (Hab. 2:4). As we grow, however, our tasks in these areas change. Spiritual growth has stages and levels of development (1 John 2:12–14).

— God deals with us where we are and shows us our next step of growth. Choose one or two of the basic requirements of life listed above. Describe where you are now in terms of the spiritual growth you see in yourself as you look back over your life.

— What do you see as your next step of growth? Make that a topic of prayer this week, asking God both to show you and to prepare you to obey him.

• *Failure:* We sin and fail in many ways. In fact, failure is inevitable, and failure is our fault and our problem.

— Several spiritual growth approaches try to resolve this dilemma. Which of these (listed below) have you been taught? Which are you following either by choice or by default?

• We don't have to fail; we can always be "victorious in Jesus" be making him truly Lord of our lives. The person who fails has not totally surrendered to God.

• The presence of sin is a sign of spiritual immaturity. It is not a surrender issue, but a growth issue.

- Failure isn't so bad, and sin and mistakes don't carry a lot of moral weight.

- Though we fail, it is not really our fault. It is the fault of others who have made us what we are: our parents, hurtful relationships, society, the Devil, or even God himself.

— It is a pretty desperate situation to realize that we must fail, that we often choose to fail, that our failure is a bad thing, and that we are held accountable. But the good news is that this dilemma leads us straight into the arms of Jesus. What failure(s) sent you into Jesus' arms initially?

— We sin in thought, word, and deed (Gal. 5:19–21; Eph. 4:31; Col. 3:5). We fail because of our ignorance (Acts 17:30). We fail because of weakness (Heb. 4:15). What growth can we experience when we acknowledge our failures and confess our sin (1 John 1:9)?

— What issues related to failure are you dealing with right now? What are you going to do to resolve those matters? Who will support you?

- **Repentance:** Learn to expect failure—and then deal with failure as Peter did, by repenting. When we sin and stop obeying, we then obey by repenting. Repentance brings forth more growth, love, responsibility, and fulfillment.

— Repentance is *a change of direction*. It is a movement away from the destructive path back toward God's way—and it requires a great deal of humility, because we have to admit we are wrong. In what aspect(s) of your life are you currently on a destructive path rather than following God's way?

Repentance involves the whole person—mind, heart, and behavior. What will repenting of the sin(s) you just acknowledged involve? Address your mind, your heart, and your behavior. Such repentance that becomes a way of life is the way to deal with any and all failures in spiritual growth.

SOURCES OF OBEDIENCE (Page 289)

Obedience requires an object—that is, we need to know what and whom to obey. There are several sources to help us with our obedience.

- **Biblical Commands:** The Ten Commandments (Ex. 20:3–17) and Jesus' two Great Commandments (Matt. 22:36–40) sum up the law, and Scripture contains many more specific principles.

   — What specific commands do you struggle to obey?

   — What are two or three ways you struggle to love God with all that you are? What are two or three ways you struggle to love your neighbor as yourself?

   — What principle for conducting your life have you recently been reminded of in your Bible study? What are you doing in response to that reminder?

- **The Holy Spirit:** God's indwelling Spirit not only brings verses to light for us to obey, but also directs those who seek his guidance to specific obedience (Mark 13:11).

  — When have you been aware of God's Spirit using a specific verse to prompt your obedience? Describe the situation and your response to the Spirit's nudge as well as the consequences of your choice to obey or disobey.

  — For what current situation would you be wise to seek the Spirit's guidance regarding what your obedience should look like? Spend some time in prayer now.

- **Authorities:** Growth has a hierarchy of authority. We should follow the leadership of church leaders and teachers, for example, as long as it is biblically appropriate.

  — If you are in church leadership as a pastor, elder, deacon, or Bible study or Sunday school teacher, why is this truth sobering?

  — When has God used one of his people in leadership to give you helpful insights and suggestions?

  — What authority problems or disobedience are you dealing with right now? What would be a good way to address them? What will be your first step, and when will you take it?

- ***Friends:*** God speaks to us in safe relationships through which he may direct us to confront an issue, deal with a problem, or confess some brokenness.

  — When have you been able to offer someone a safe friendship where he or she felt free to confront an issue, deal with a problem, or confess some brokenness? In what ways did that experience affect your relationship with the Lord?

  — When has God used a friend to give you a safe place to confront an issue, deal with a problem, or confess some brokenness? What growth resulted from that experience?

  — What issue, problem, or brokenness are you facing now? What friend could God use to help you? When will you go to that friend—or when will you take the first step toward finding a person who might support you?

- ***Circumstantial Leading:*** Be aware that God may arrange events to direct you. Attend to the possible interpretations of what is happening in your life. This should be done in consultation with a wise mentor, counselor, or pastor.

  — When have you appreciated in hindsight God's choreography of the events of your life? Describe what he arranged and how he moved you to where he wanted you to be.

  — What current circumstances have you wondering if God is directing you in a certain direction? With whom will you discuss the possible significance of these circumstances?

These five different sources of obedience are not in conflict or fragmented. If you sense conflicts in the above areas and you don't know how to obey, ask God to help you find his voice among the many.

TASKS FOR THE GROWER (Page 290)

The person who is growing needs to understand the importance of obedience. Here are a few of the essential tasks for the grower.

- ***Surrender to the Lordship of Christ:*** The more you surrender your life to God's authority and care, the more you are living life as you were designed to.

  — Note your progress toward making God the center of your life. Where is he Lord where he wasn't before?

  — Name one or two areas of your life that need to come more fully under God's authority and care.

- ***Follow Him Daily:*** Look at obedience as a daily and continuous process.

  — What are you doing—or could you be doing—to keep your heart more attentive to what God might be saying to you in the Bible, by the Spirit, from his people, or in circumstances?

  — Who offers you support in this daily and continuous process of obedience—or where might you go to find such support?

- ***Deal with Your Character Issues:*** One of the outworkings of a decision to obey God is learning about your character weaknesses and dealing with them.

  — Dealing with character weaknesses means owning your perfectionism, confessing the insecurity and pride that drive it, working on being accepted as you are, being honest with others about your frailties, and letting go of being a perfect person, which has protected you from self-criticism and condemnation. Which of these traits—or others that came to mind as you read the list—are issues you need to address?

  — What will "dealing with" these character weaknesses involve? Be sure to include the key role that obedience plays in dealing with character weaknesses.

RESPONSIBILITIES OF THE HELPER (Page 291)

People who are helping others grow can do several things to make obedience an integral part of the process.

- ***Position Obedience as Encompassing All of Life:*** In what ways is obedience to God relevant to your daily life? Be specific.

- ***Teach Obedience as Bringing Good to People:*** When have you seen (in your life or someone else's) obedience leading to a better, richer, and less dysfunctional life? What change to obedience from current disobedience would lead you to a better, richer, and less dysfunctional life?

- ***Deal with Outside and Inside:*** In what areas of life is your obedience devotional and externalized? In what areas does your obedience extend only to emotional growth? What absolute parameters of the Bible are you ignoring? In what ways are you addressing obedience of the heart as well as adhering to scriptural standards of life?

Obedience, or God-directedness, is a lifelong process central to spiritual growth. Stay close to what God says regarding your ways, relationships, and inner issues. When we learn the ways of obedience, we enter the path of growth. Yet that path is not without danger. We need to understand how to handle the problems of sin and temptation, as we discover in the next chapter.

> *Lord God, obedience sounds so simple, but this is anything but easy! Help me, Lord, to be more God-directed and less self-directed. Teach me to look to you as naturally as I breathe. And help me to continue to surrender to you those areas of my life and aspects of myself where I still want to be in charge. God, I want to surrender more fully to the lordship of Christ; I want to follow him daily; and I want to deal openly with my character weaknesses so that you may grow me to be more like Christ, in whose name I pray. Amen.*

TIPS FOR GROWERS:

- Realize that obedience is more than simply adhering to specific commands. Instead, it is a way of life that will bring you good fruit and success. Understand, too, the nature of both external and internal obedience. When you encounter a personal struggle, look at these two dimensions of obedience to see what is awry.

- Ask God to show you what your specific growth tasks of obedience are: surrendering to the lordship of Christ, following him daily, or dealing with your character issues.

- See the reality of falling from obedience as normal. Explain why the processes of confession and repentance get you back on track.

- Look at obedience relationally. In what ways is your life of obedience or disobedience affecting God and people? What obedience would help you to be more fully reconciled to God and others?

CHAPTER SIXTEEN

Pulling the Weeds: The Problem of Sin and Temptation

The Bible teaches not only that we are responsible and accountable for our sin, but that we are powerless to keep from sinning. We cannot change, and we are held responsible for not being able to change. Anyone need a Savior?

- Paul wrote, "I have the desire to do what is good, but I cannot carry it out. For what I do is not the good I want to do; no, the evil I do not want to do—this I keep on doing" (Rom. 7:18–19). When have you realized that truth about yourself— the truth that you cannot do the good you want to do and that you keep doing the evil you don't want to do? Give two or three recent examples.

- We are responsible and accountable for our sin, but we cannot do anything about it in a fully significant or sufficient way. When have you realized that "just making better choices" is not effective against your compulsive behavior or an internal character problem or sin?

Trying to "do better" does not work, so we need help because our sin is hurting us or someone else. Help has come in the form of the gospel. The goal of this chapter is to give a few thoughts on how the problem of sin works in our lives and how the gospel is the answer to this problem in all areas of growth.

FIRST, A WARNING (Page 296)

In a discussion of personal growth, when we say that sin is a problem, we are not saying that a person's individual sin is the cause of all the struggles or problems he or she might have.

- Job, like all of us, lived in a fallen world where there is suffering we cannot understand. What struggles or problems in your life are examples of suffering you just don't understand?

- People suffer because of the sin of others. What struggles or problems in your life have come because of the sin of others?

- Everyone suffers and sometimes lacks growth for other reasons besides his or her own sin. Have you failed to understand this and blamed yourself for your suffering—or has someone else failed to understand this truth about suffering and blamed you for the pain you're in? Describe the situation in healthier terms—that is, without crediting the circumstances to your sin.

Again, as we look at the subject of sin, let's first understand that everyone suffers and sometimes lacks growth for other reasons besides his or her sin.

WHAT DOESN'T WORK (Page 297)

We would like to start this chapter with a brief reminder of what the "law of sin and death" is about and why it doesn't work.

- Being "under the law" is the system of having a commandment and then choosing to follow that commandment to be good and acceptable, or not following the commandment and being condemned. Part of the problem is that we are no longer free, in ourselves, to do the right thing, no matter how much we want to. Now we possess a "sinful nature" (Rom. 7:5). We have a penchant for doing unhelpful things as well as sometimes doing downright destructive things. And not only do we have a passion for doing those things that are against the law, but the law itself arouses in us a passion to do the very thing we shouldn't do (Rom. 7:5, 8–10)!

  — What evidence of your "sinful nature" is apparent in your life?

  — What unhelpful things do you have a penchant for doing? Be specific.

  — When has the passion for doing those things that are against the law been aroused within you by the law itself? Put differently, when has your heavenly Father's "no" almost seemed to make you do that wrong thing?

- As a solution to the sin problem, Christians may offer harsh, angry preaching against sin with the injunction to repent; legalistic rules to keep people in line; or the message that the "way" out is to make better choices.

  — Which of these have you encountered? And which of these have you offered to a hurting, sinning fellow believer?

— These three options produce guilt (condemnation), anger (rebellion), and fear. Which of these options did you experience as a result of the counsel you just mentioned receiving? (And, as far as you know, which of these options did the person you counseled experience?)

— If we just tell people to do right and don't give them the whole gospel, we reap results we are not looking for: failure and bad feelings. Explain why the sharing of the "whole gospel" (Rom. 1:17; 8:6; 2 Tim. 1:10) leads to different results.

Dirk had the standard for losing weight; he had the law, the "should." He made a commitment to lose weight, he failed, and then he felt guilty and condemned. As a result, he gained instead of lost weight. Then he would repeat the cycle. This is a good picture of law and sin at work.

A BETTER WAY: REPENTANCE AND LIVING BY THE SPIRIT (Page 299)

The Bible gives us a better way: While the law (and all of our versions of it) cannot help, Jesus can (Rom. 8:3–4). He replaces living by the law with living by the Spirit. This means living according to a relationship and a process that empowers us (Gal. 5:16, 25). So we are once again back to dependency on God.

• To change the areas we want to change, we have to first admit to them (confession) and then admit we are unable to change them by ourselves. Next we have to be set free by establishing a relationship with Jesus, which takes care of the guilt and condemnation of the law. Then we must live according to the Spirit. Here is where most failure takes place.

— Turn to page 300 of the text and review the list of things we need to ask God to do for us through his Spirit. Which of these do you pray about regularly?

— What difference in your spiritual growth might such prayer make?

— Which item(s) listed will you begin to incorporate in your prayers?

• When we admit powerlessness, ask God and others for help, repent, continue to stay plugged into a supportive environment, seek healing for the hurting parts of ourselves, receive deep forgiveness, give that to others, and obey God—when we do all these things, then long-standing patterns of problematic behavior change. This is the way the Bible has described the process we need.

— When have you, consciously or not, followed this process? What long-standing behavior changed?

— What problematic behavior would you like to change? What will you do today to begin the process of change?

We cannot stop sinning; we have to be *saved* from sin (Luke 19:10). The biblical process of overcoming sin provides a deep healing. Anything else will fall short. *So the Bible's commandment regarding sin is and always has been: Repent.*

REBELLION (Page 301)

Lest we become a little too comfortable in our "we are just sick and powerless and want to be healed" thinking, we need to look at another side of sin. We are sometimes very able to keep from sinning, and we choose not to. We rebel, as Adam and Eve did *before* they had a sin nature.

- Slowly Joe changed as the "life in the Spirit" took hold. More and more he became the loving husband Sara had desired. But during a difficult weekend, Joe chose to be mean instead of restraining himself. This was not a case of weakness. It was a choice, and it was nothing but ugly sin.

  — Sometimes we are unable to do what we are supposed to do at any given moment. In those areas we need more work of the Sprit and need to flee the temptation and run to get help. What can you ask God to do for you through his Spirit in these situations? Review the list on page 300 of the text. And where (or to whom) can you go for help when you need to flee temptation? Have a specific spot or two—or a person or a useful Scripture passage or a place to pray—in mind so that you're prepared when temptation arises.

  — At other times we do not use the abilities we do possess and we willingly, willfully choose to sin. Confess those willful sins in your life (Ps. 19:13). When are you especially susceptible to willful sins? What can you do to stand strong and/or to escape those vulnerable situations? What will you do to teach yourself to say "don't do that" to yourself?

  — A lot is going on in the name of growth today that is just sin in need of repentance. Are you playing that game? If so, the solution is confession, remorse, repentance, making amends, and reconciliation. What sin do you need to confess? That's the first step toward genuine growth.

Confronted with the reality that he could choose to sin, Joe had a new dimension to his growth—the realization that he now had more freedom and, with it, more responsibility.

NO EXCUSES (Page 304)

Blame is part of the natural order of fallen humankind. We do not "own" our behavior; instead, we automatically shift responsibility. To the extent that we continue in blame and continue to explain our sin away, the Bible says we will die. Sin kills us, and blame gives life to sin.

- Blaming is human.
  - When have you blamed someone for your behavior rather than taking responsibility for it? Give a specific example.

  - What sin did that blame give life to?

  - Who are you blaming now for some aspect of your behavior? What sin is resulting from that blame?

- Getting to the root of what motivates our behavior is very important. Many motivations or driving forces are not our fault. But this does not mean that our behavior is not our responsibility. Our background does not explain or justify why we choose to deal destructively with our hurt.
  - When have you used or been tempted to use what happened to you in your past to explain away your behavior?

  - What choice is involved in dealing with past hurts? See Romans 12:17 and 21.

   — What responsibility are you avoiding by staying focused on the past? What will you do to let go of the past? What will you do to take on the responsibility that is rightfully yours?

A spiritual response to hurt and anger would be to submit to the healing process described above and work it out without returning "evil for evil." When dealing with our own hurt, lacks, and other motivators of behavior, we have to remember that there is a difference between what happens to us and how we deal with it.

SIN IS MORE THAN EXTERNAL DEEDS (Page 306)

Too often we think of sin only in external, not internal, terms. But it is important to deal with internal motivations. Unresolved anger and hurt, for instance, can turn into bitterness or lust. Hatred for authority can ruin careers. And many other monsters lurk in the human breast.

- Looking inside ourselves and resolving the issues we find there is the key to having the outside be good. If we are full of "crummy stuff," we will exhibit crummy behavior; the same holds for good stuff.

   — Jesus offered quite a list of the bad that can issue from the human heart: "evil thoughts, sexual immorality, theft, murder, adultery, greed, malice, deceit, lewdness, envy, slander, arrogance and folly" (Mark 7:21–22). Which of these have you been guilty of?

   — What has resulted from these motivators? Illness, failure, addictions, relationship difficulties, and destructive behaviors are some of the possibilities.

   — Which of the bad that Jesus listed are you involved in now? What is resulting from that involvement? Why are you staying involved in the bad?

- The truth is that all of us have crummy stuff within us. It is, in Jesus' words, the "sickness" of sin (Mark 2:17). If we are ever going to get well, we have to have the safety to look inside, confess what we find there, grieve it, repent of it, and "put off [our] old self, which is being corrupted by its deceitful desires" (Eph. 4:22).

  — Being made new from the inside out begins when we face how ugly things are inside. What inside ugliness are you aware of?

  — Where or to whom can you safely say, "You won't believe how sick I am! Let me tell you about this thought I had today"?

When we recognize the internal aspect of our sin and confess that sin, we can begin to clean up our insides.

FROM MORALLY NEUTRAL TO MORALLY BAD (Page 307)

Not only the ugly stuff can lead us to sin.

- Unresolved hurt, for instance, can tempt a person to sin. The hurt is not the sin. *The sin is the way that the person deals with the pain and emptiness.* It is the result of trying to meet a valid need in a sinful way.

  — Give an example (ideally from your own life) of an attempt to meet a valid need in a sinful way.

  — What valid need are you currently trying to meet in a sinful way? What is a better way to meet that need? When will you start choosing that way?

- The world has its solutions to need and pain, and we can all be tempted to resolve our hurts with worldly solutions. *Sin is failing to depend on God and not saying yes to his grace in all its various forms.* Meeting our needs our way is idolatry and never works.

  — When have you tried to resolve your hurts or meet your needs with the world's solutions, giving in at a weak moment to the lust of the flesh, the lure of power, the boastful pride of life, the lust of the eyes, and/or the lure of materialism (1 John 2:15–16)? What resulted when you tried one of the world's solutions?

  — Which one of these solutions are you currently turning to in your attempt to re-solve some hurt or meet a need?

  — What form(s) of God's grace can help you stand strong against the world's tempt-ing but false solutions to needs and hurts? When will you turn from the world's false solution and receive that grace?

- *Overcoming sin is never just about doing away with badness; it is always also about adding goodness.* Jesus came to do away with death, but he also came to give us life. Therefore we need to respond to sin by looking beyond the sin nature to what is motivating and driving the sin.

  — What has motivated and driven your sin? Give an example or two.

  — Sin is driven and perpetuated by being cut off from "the life of God" (Eph. 4:18–19). The life of God includes, among other things, support, connection, honesty, healing, confession, repentance, correction, and discipline. Which of these, had they been in place, might have helped you avoid the sin you just acknowledged?

— Which of the goods just listed are you experiencing today? Which do you need to add to your life? Which item will be the first? What will you do?

Some of what is behind "badness" is not so bad after all. It is a well of good needs and hurt and pain that people try to "medicate" in bad ways. Instead, we need to take care of our needs and our pains that are not connected to the life of God.

AVOIDING SIN (Page 309)

Temptation is all around. The Bible has a strategy for avoiding it.

- **Pray:** When his disciples asked him to teach them to pray, Jesus included, "And lead us not into temptation, but deliver us from the evil one" (Matt. 6:13). Do you take your sin seriously enough to pray consistently to avoid it? If not, why not? What sin do you need to be praying about?

- **Flee and Escape:** Paul taught that "God will not let you be tempted beyond what you can bear. But when you are tempted, he will also provide a way out" (1 Cor. 10:13). Do you consciously and consistently choose to avoid those situations where you know you will be tempted to sin? If not, why do you flirt with sin?

Get away from tempting things *before* the temptation, not after. If you are not there, you can't be tempted. And when you find yourself in danger, don't just stand there and try to win. Instead, run from it.

REMEMBERING WHAT SIN IS (Page 311)

We are tempted to forget what sin actually is. Remember that God created humankind to be connected to him in specific roles. We were to be in relationship and under his lordship, staying in our role as creature. But we tried to usurp God's role and become our own god. And that is basically what sin is, to live independent of God.

• Sin always appears as independence from God and a taking over and usurping of his roles. What independence from God are you guilty of?

• When there is sin in our life, we are likely to find problems in the areas listed below.

Independence—trying to meet our own needs apart from God and his people

Loss of relationship—isolation from God and others

Boss—not submitting to God and obeying him

Control—trying to control others or things, resulting in a loss of self-control and A failure to yield to God's sovereign control

Judging—of self and others

Self-rule—trying to design life on your own terms

Which of these problem areas do you see in your life? Confess those sins and repent of them now.

Don't get confused by the distraction that individual acts of sin can cause. There is a deeper sickness that only humbling oneself before God can cure. When we do so, relationship is restored, and we once again become who we were created to be, humans and not gods.

ONE MORE NOTE (Page 311)

• We can't deal with sin and temptation without confession and repentance. They are assumed in everything this chapter addresses. Make sure you include confession and repentance in your understanding of all that this chapter discusses.

THE TWO GREATEST COMMANDMENTS (Page 312)

Jesus said that all the commandments rest on the two great commandments of loving God and loving your neighbor as yourself. What exactly do these two commandments have to do with dealing with sin?

* First, to love God means that we obey him as well as do things his way. What sins of yours would you avoid if you simply (and we know it isn't easy!) obeyed God's commands and principles?

* Second, loving others can cure our own problems as well.
  — Review why loving others (specifically, his wife and children) would help Dirk deal with his own sin.

  — Think about your own sin (addictions, lust, irresponsibility, etc.) and its effect on people you love. As you do so, what motivation do you find for conquering your sin?

Think of how your behavior is affecting other people, and that will motivate you to stop when rules won't. Remember, all the Law and the Prophets rest on the ultimate Law of Love.

GOOD OLD-FASHIONED RELIGION (Page 313)

As you read this chapter, it might seem a little strange to hear so much about sin from psychologists. Well, we strongly believe that if any one of us is going to grow personally, we must deal with our own sin as well as the sin of others. For those are the two ways that sin affects our lives: sin by us and sin done to us.

- The formula for dealing with sin we commit has been around for a long time: confession, forgiveness, and repentance. With repentance comes a turning to the life of God and a filling up of the soul with the "good stuff" of his life.

  — What sin is God calling you to address?

  — With what "good stuff" are you filling your soul?

- The formula for dealing with the sin done to us is similar: confession, granting forgiveness, healing the wounds through God's life, and reconciliation, if possible.

  — What sin done to you is still unresolved?

  — When will you take the first (or the next) step to resolve it?

- Both kinds of sin require the grace of God, facing the truth about oneself or others, receiving the life we need, receiving and granting forgiveness, and reconciling as much as we can. What support do you have for taking these steps, some of which are quite difficult?

There are no new ways of dealing with sin, for God gave us the Way a long time ago. The gospel is the medicine for the sickness we all possess, and that really is good news.

Lord God, I am indeed in a bad situation: I'm responsible and accountable for my sin, but I am powerless to keep from sinning. (Your law even makes me want to sin more!) I can't change, and yet you'll hold me responsible for not being able to change. I am so glad for the good news of gospel, for the fact that Jesus can help me. So, Jesus, I ask you to save me and to help me learn to live by the Spirit. Show me where I am trying to live independent of you, and work in me so that my life is characterized by love for you and love for others, that I might avoid sin and glorify you. I pray in Jesus' name. Amen.

TIPS FOR GROWERS:

- See yourself as both powerless over and responsible for your sin. Die to any model of thinking that says willpower will suffice. Get rid of the law in your life and the cycle of trying harder, failing, condemning yourself, and then trying harder. Instead, practice living by the Spirit.

- Recognize the seriousness of your sin and its destructiveness. Take responsibility for your sin—honestly and squarely. Identify the ways you have denied how sin keeps you from experiencing all you want to have in life and with God and other people. Yet also realize that your personal sin is not the cause of everything bad in your life, because you live in a fallen world and other people's sin can cause bad things in your life.

- Fight against sin not just with willpower or leaning on God, but relying on all that he gives us in the life of the Spirit. Ask yourself where you are not avoiding or fleeing temptation. In addition, have an overall orientation toward repentance.

- Take a deeper view of sin—as in chapter 2—whereby you see the effects of original sin and how it is operating in your life. See where you have disconnected from God as the Source of life, God as the Boss, relationship as primary, and the roles human beings are supposed to play. Also, address the needs and deprivations driving some sins. Identify where you are separated from the life of God.

CHAPTER SEVENTEEN

Facing Reality: How Truth Deepens Growth

Although we don't always receive it graciously, truth is one of God's essential tools for growing us up, and he gives us many types of needed truth from different sources.

- When have you been hurt by truth not spoken in love—and when have you hurt someone by speaking truth but not doing so in love?

- Are you afraid of truth? If so, why—and exactly what do you fear?

Truth is sometimes painful, but it is always our friend, because it comes from the Lord, whose love and truth protect us (Ps. 40:11). He dispenses it to us out of a heart of compassion and grace. Like anything else from God, truth works *for* us, not *against* us.

WHAT IS TRUTH? (Page 318)

Truth is what is; truth is reality, what exists. Something can be truly good (like love) or truly bad (like deception), but both are part of the truth. Conversely, what doesn't exist can't be true even if we want it to be.

- A person might want to see herself as not having selfish parts (a bad true thing) but instead as being a totally giving person (a good untrue thing). We sometimes try to squeeze reality and truth into our own framework. This always fails.

  — What "bad true thing" about yourself would you like to ignore?

  — What "good untrue thing" have you believed or been tempted to believe about yourself?

  — Why is it hard to see and accept the truth about yourself?

- Biblical scholars have categorized truth in different ways to help with the bigness of the concept. "Ontological" truth refers to all of reality, and "propositional" truth is a set of integrated statements about that reality. Another important classification of truth is revelation, special revelation (the truths of the Bible) as well as general revelation (the realities of observed life). Attending to both types helps us learn what is good for our lives.

  — What has God's special revelation taught you about what is good for your life, especially right now? List two or three things.

  — What has God's general revelation shown you about what is good for your life, specifically for circumstances you currently face? Again, give two or three examples.

THE MANY FACETS OF TRUTH (Page 319)

The Bible uses the word *truth* to describe different aspects of reality as well as what is true in general (1 Tim. 2:7).

- The first reality is that of God himself. God is called "the God of truth" (Ps. 31:15). Jesus calls himself the Way, the Truth, and the Life (John 14:6). The Holy Spirit is also called the Truth (1 John 5:6). Why is it significant that the triune God you worship and serve is a God of truth?

- Since truth is part of God's nature and since we are made in his image, we are not only to know truth, but we are to experience it. Describe a time when you have had an emotional as well as an intellectual grasp of God's truth.

- The Scriptures refer to themselves as a whole as the truth (Ps. 119:43; 2 Tim. 2:15), and Jesus affirms this (John 17:17). When we read the Bible, we expose ourselves to God's truths of life and growth. Tell of a time from your own life when the Bible's revelation of God's truth spoke directly to you.

- The Bible says that people who are aligned with truth are honest and righteous. We are to think on whatever is true, noble, and right (Phil. 4:8); love "rejoices in the truth" (1 Cor. 13:6). And people who love truthfulness instead of falsehood are living right. What evidence that you are living right, that you are aligned with truth, and/or that you rejoice in the truth could someone find in your life? Be specific.

- Finally, the Bible uses the word *truth* to refer to the specific body of facts regarding Jesus' atoning death for us, which reconciles us to God (Eph. 1:13). Take a minute now to practice explaining the gospel truth to someone who knows nothing about Jesus or about her own need for a Savior.

Truth is many things to God, but these many things do not conflict with one another. Truth is always consistent with itself, as God cannot be a part of lies (Titus 1:2).

- **Its Sources:** We can find truth in many places. God uses them all to help us grow in him. Note how he has used or, better, is currently using each of the following to grow you.

His Spirit and presence (1 John 5:6)

The Bible (2 Tim. 3:16)

People (Prov. 15:31)

Your conscience (1 Tim. 1:19)

Circumstances (1 Cor. 10:1–6)

WHAT TRUTH DOES (Page 320)

- **Truth Provides a Path for Life:** To mature, people need a path or guide. Truth is that path (Ps. 119:30); it provides a structure for the process of growth. With God's truth as a guide, we can know how to order our steps. Consider, for instance, how the commands to love God and your neighbor (Matt. 22:38–39) can govern your everyday life as well as your long-term plans.

— What do these commands say to you about the nitty-gritty of your life today? Be specific.

— What do these commands say to you about your life for the long-term? Again, be specific.

- ***Truth Is Married to Love and Grace:*** When love is separated from truth, love cannot grow.

  — In what ways is your love not being honest? Why?

  — When has the truth you've spoken not been for the other person's best? Why was that the case?

- ***Truth Saves and Gives Life:*** Truth both preserves and provides a life for us. It protects us, and it also guides us into life-giving activities and relationships.

  — When has truth protected you by warning you of a danger? What danger are you currently protected from because of your knowledge of God's truth?

— When have you sensed the life-giving power of Scripture? For what one aspect of your life do you currently need Scripture's life-giving power? What are you doing to receive that power? With whom are you seeking Scripture's life-giving truth?

— And when have you gone to a trusted friend with struggles, dreams, or desires and found life in that relationship? What friendship offers you that refuge now?

- ***Truth Separates What Is Real and What Is Not:*** Truth helps us clarify the real and not-so-real (Heb. 4:12).

  — When, for instance, has the truth (what is real) about a situation enabled you to solve a problem?

  — What current situation might you not be seeing the truth about? Who can be a truth-speaker in your life? When will you contact that person?

When truth is hidden, many problems can arise. When we learn that truth is our friend, growth happens.

TRUTHS IMPORTANT TO SPIRITUAL GROWTH (Page 322)

Several truths are important to the spiritual growth process. As you learn these truths, you'll see in your life the fruit of spiritual growth.

- ***The Truth of God's Design:*** We need to know that God has designed a structure for our spiritual growth that will give us a good life (Jer. 29:11).

— When have you seen the truth of God's plan for growth (for example, seeking him, being poor in spirit, taking ownership of one's life) bear fruit in your life or someone else's?

— What aspect of God's plan for growth are you currently involved in? Describe your efforts.

- **The Truth of Our Condition:** Everyone has weaknesses, sins, immaturities, and brokenness. We all have to grow.

  — What particular issues of growth do you need to deal with?

  — Which areas of your life need God's healing and maturing?

  — In what areas are you fragile, or where do you notice a pattern of failure? What will you do to address these?

- **The Truth of Our Resources:** Spiritual growth requires certain ingredients to work correctly. Some of those are:

  A spiritual context where God is seen as central to growth
  Abiding, loving, and truthful human relationships
  Experience and competence in growth

Enough time for the process to take hold
A structure or framework that fits the needs of the growers

— Which of these ingredients are very present in your life—and which of these resources for growth do you need to add?

- ***The Truth of the Tasks Required:*** Whatever people are working on, they need to know what activities bring about the fruit of growth. We need not only know the truth about ourselves, but we need also to act on it (James 1:22–25).

  — Currently, what truth(s) about yourself are you acting on? Cite one or two.

  — Which one or two truths about yourself are you not yet acting on? Why not?

- ***The Truth of the Obstacles to Growth:*** Everyone in spiritual growth needs to be aware of the problems he or she will face in the process. Keep in mind that the struggles we encounter sometimes mean we're doing something right.

  — What have you learned about the wiles of Satan—and what will you do to learn more?

  — What are you recognizing about the resistance to growth in your own heart?

— And what problems with people are you encountering as you become more of a person of light?

THE KINDS OF TRUTH WE NEED FOR GROWTH (Page 323)

Truth plays several roles in our lives. Here are some of the principal ways truth leads to growth.

- *Illumination:* God brings all sorts of truth to us to help us see how best to handle life.

  — What dark part of your life, for instance, has God been exposing recently? What issue has God recently shown you?

  — When has a good Bible study brought illumination? Or when have you had a flash of insight as to what was driving a problem in your life?

  — What character pattern or situation in your life can you ask God to illuminate for you?

- *Comfort:* Comfort is the emotional supply we receive from God and others and then pass on to those who need it to bear the pains of life.

  — When have you been comforted by someone who understands your pain and struggle at a deep level and communicates that understanding to you?

— When has God used you to give that kind of comfort to someone else?

— For what do you need this kind of comfort now? Or to whom can you extend that kind of comfort? In either case, when will you reach out?

- ***Clarification:*** We need to understand which of our struggles are our fault, which are the result of someone else's sin, and which are the result of living in a broken world. We need to clarify what is our problem in a relationship and what is not.

— Tell of a time when clarification showed you how to resolve a particular issue.

— For what current struggle would you like clarification? To whom can you go?

- ***Guidance:*** Sometimes the truth gives us a direction to take in our growth and life (Ps. 119:105).

— When has the application of one of God's general principles (the law of empathy [Luke 6:31] or the principle of seeking God's kingdom first [Matt. 6:33], for instance) enabled you to unravel a life issue?

— When has God provided individual and specific guidance to you through, for example, a nudging of the Spirit, a Scripture passage that applied to your situation, or the advice of a trusted friend?

— For what situation or life issue are you currently asking God's guidance? Through what Bible studies and/or relationships might God guide you?

- **Correction:** We need to be confronted with truth when we stray from God's path. In fact, it is sad but true that we always need to be receptive to correction.

  — What keeps you from being receptive to correction? If being receptive to correction comes easily, what's your secret?

  — Through what Bible studies and/or relationships might God offer you correction?

HOW WE SHOULD APPROACH TRUTH (Page 326)

Here are some stances that can best maximize the healing, growing effects of truth.

- **Love Truth:** When people understand that truth can save and preserve their lives, it is hard not to love it. So seek God's truth. Hunt it down. And hang around honest people.

  — Do you struggle to love truth? If so, describe your experience of truth divorced from love or, if you've known more permissiveness than truth, your conclusion that truth has little value.

  — When have you seen that, although not always comfortable, truth helps our lives become more of what they were designed to be?

— What will you do in practical terms to seek God's truth, to hunt it down? Be specific.

- ***Endure the Pain of Truth:*** Truth is often hurtful and uncomfortable. Like the surgeon's knife, its healing power comes with pain.
    — When have you had to endure the pain of truth? Why were you able to endure that pain?

    — Note which of the following painful experiences you have faced. Then describe the growth or fruit that resulted.

    Facing the reality of your failings

    Living life God's way instead of how you would like to live it

    Loving others when you are aware of their imperfections

    Having truthful conversations with people you love

    Holding on to your values when others judge you wrongly

    Learning new ways to conduct relationships that are not easy or natural for you

— Which of these painful experiences are you currently facing? What are you doing to ensure that growth or fruit will result?

• ***Recognize How Love Helps the Pain:*** The more love we internalize, the more truth we can bear. Love gives us the support and grace to tolerate difficult realities.

— Do you find that truth hurts too much? (If not, thank God for your support base. It's doing its job!) If truth does hurt too much, you may need to increase or deepen your support base. What steps can you take toward that end?

— As we are loved more, we also see things about ourselves—our brokenness and our sins—more and more clearly. When, if at all, have you experienced this reality in your own life? What did you realize about yourself?

— As we are loved more, we just don't go into bad places when people we trust tell us the hard truth about ourselves. When have you been able to trust "wounds from a friend" (Prov. 27:6)?

• ***Be Sensitive to Truth and Untruth:*** The more a person takes a stance toward truthfulness, the more discerning he becomes about truth and untruth. Darkness and light become more distinct from each other (John 1:5).

— When have you noticed a sensitivity to truth and untruth that you realized was new to you? Why was that sensitivity a good thing?

— What can you do to take a stronger stance toward truthfulness?

- ***Be Receptive to All Styles of Truth:*** Be receptive to all types of reality. Some people, for example, understand linear, logical truth more easily, while others do better with intuition.
  - Are you more logical or intuitive? Support your answer with an example or two from your life.

  - Consider one or two people with whom you are in close relationship. Could some of the sparks between you, however rare, be due to the fact that your cognitive styles are different? If so, why might this insight help strengthen your relationship?

- ***Learn to Live with Mystery and the Unknown Truths:*** In spiritual growth we need to learn to live with what we do not, and sometimes can never, know. God alone knows all truth, as he alone can bear the weight of it.
  - Which of the following unknowns are you having to accept, live with, and move on from?

    All facts about your childhood and past
    Reasons people in your life did the things they did
    Reasons you did everything you have done
    Why God allowed certain things to happen
    Exactly when you will be through with a particular issue

— When are you going to accept, live with, and move on from the unknowns you just identified?

— Why is it a blessing that we don't have the answers to all our questions?

CONCLUSION (Page 331)

You don't have to be afraid of the truth, even when it hurts. Seek reality and become a person of the truth.

- Look back at the beginning of the chapter and the reasons you noted for being afraid of truth. What truths in this chapter have eased at least some of that fear? Pray about any remaining fear and share it with a safe person you can trust.

- In your own words, explain why it is important to become a person of the truth.

- What are you doing to become a person of truth?

The next chapter, dealing with activity, will help you to take initiative in that process of seeking truth and growing as a result.

Lord God, truth is always a friend because it comes from you. Help me be a lover of truth. Teach me to be a seeker of truth. And strengthen me with the reassurance of your love for me as I learn to accept hard truths about my-self. I want to live in the light of your truth and love. I pray in the name of Jesus, who said, "I am the Way and the Truth and the Life" (John 14:6). Amen.

TIPS FOR GROWERS:

- Consider whether you experience truth as harsh, critical, and condemning. Teach yourself to see truth as a giver of life and as your friend.

- Look for ways to internalize truth. Consider learning Scripture, being sensitive to the promptings of the Spirit, being in relationship with safe people, and discerning what God is doing through your life circumstances. See truth as connecting you to people and leading you to growth.

- Become aware of your resistance to certain types of truth. For example, some people are more comfortable dealing with the truth about their hurt and weakness, but are averse to facing the truth about their selfishness and rebellion.

- Learn both to receive and to give truth graciously and humbly. Recognize the value of making truthfulness a part of all your relationships.

CHAPTER EIGHTEEN

Putting on the Gloves: The Importance of Activity

O ver time, I (John) noticed two major differences between Glenn and Anne. First, they differed in the degree to which they struggled with character issues and, second, in the degree to which they sought spiritual growth.

- Are you more like Glenn or Anne? Be specific about the character traits, the background details, and the commitment (or lack of commitment) to spiritual growth you share with one or the other. Support your answer with evidence from your life.

- In the case of Glenn and Anne, the person with more damage to her soul grew more than the person who was less damaged. What are some possible reasons for that?

The real difference between Glenn and Anne was their level of active involvement in the growth process.

GOD WORKS, WE WORK (PAGE 334)

Activity—being energetically involved in an endeavor—is part of who God is and how we are made in his image.

- A good life always reflects the two dimensions of work and love. Spiritual, relational people also have meaningful, active lives of purpose. They are deeply connected emotionally and have jobs, ministries, and hobbies that make life richer.

  — Evaluate these two dimensions of your life: work and love. What job, ministry, and/or hobby makes life richer for you? With whom are you connected emotionally?

  — What will you do to strengthen each dimension of your life, to become better connected to people (love) and to be involved in meaningful activities (work)? Be specific—and then begin the process. Commit to the growth, arrange for accountability, work through your resistance, and find support for your efforts to increase your involvement in a good life.

- Activity and love are intertwined. Loving God and others is the end result and purpose of basically any good activity.

  — List three or four of your regular activities.

  — Now explain how loving God and others is both the end result and the purpose of each activity—or explain how keeping that perspective in mind would change and even redeem those activities.

Again, activity and love are intertwined. Love is the fuel of activity; love is also its purpose and goal.

SPIRITUAL GROWTH REQUIRES ACTION (Page 335)

Action is always an integral part of growth. Spiritual growth does not "happen" to us; it requires a great deal of blood, sweat, and tears. Yet this doesn't mean either that we must do it all on our own or that God does it all. Our sanctification is a collaborative effort between God and us (Phil. 2:12–13).

- At this point of the chapter (and of your life), what does it mean to you to "work out your salvation with fear and trembling"? Be specific about what you are doing (or have thought about doing) in that regard. Comment too on why the apostle Paul calls us to do this work "with fear and trembling."

- What does it mean to you that, as the book says, "we are partners in our own spiritual surgery"? What urgency or significance does this metaphor give to your role in your spiritual growth?

THE PLACE OF ACTIVITY IN GROWTH (Page 336)

When we grow spiritually, we perform many tasks. In fact, most of the time, growth requires action.

- **Reconciliation Versus Fairness:** An active stance toward growth means we give more weight to reconciliation than to fairness (Matt. 5:23–24; 18:15). After all, God himself gave up demands for fairness for the sake of relationship with us.
  — What kind of spiritual growth results from, first, giving up your demands for fairness and, second, from making efforts toward reconciliation? If you'd like, supplement your answer with details about a personal experience.

— What opportunity do you have right now to choose reconciliation instead of insisting on fairness? What might be the consequences of each? Who will support the choice of reconciliation?

- **Ownership:** When we are active in our growth, we take more responsibility for our lives. When people are passive about their growth, they let others control them and see forces outside of them as being in charge of their lives. The more you own your life, the more things change for the better.

    — Where do you think you fall on the spectrum between active and passive? Why?

    — What aspect of taking ownership of your life is threatening to you? What does the *How People Grow* text suggest about what you should do in the face of such threats?

    — What current issues in your life do you need to take ownership of? Why are you hesitant about taking responsibility for those areas? What will you do to overcome your hesitation? Who, for instance, will you ask to pray for you? Who will hold you accountable?

- **Learning from Mistakes:** When people seek to grow spiritually, they soon realize that they will be trying new ways of relating to God and others. They discover new thoughts, feelings, and parts of themselves. They don't know much about them at first, and they make many errors.

— What "new ways of relating to God and others" have you tried or considered trying since you started reading this book?

— What mistake(s) have you made or do you almost expect to make as you act on these growth principles?

— What is your attitude toward mistakes—and what is a healthy attitude?

THE TASKS OF GROWTH (Page 339)

It is important to understand what you need to do to foster your own spiritual growth. The process involves much effort but brings forth much fruit.

- *Humble Yourself Before God:* See yourself as God sees you. This position of humility helps you assume a position of need, dependency, and obedience.
    - When have life events humbled you? When has God's Word, his people, and/or your own human limitations humbled you? What growth are you aware of resulting from that?

    - What source of humbling—life events, God's Word, his people, your own limitations—are you currently experiencing? What is your response?

— Regarding what attitude do you need to humble yourself before God right now?

— What area of life could you be approaching more humbly?

- *Search for Areas That Need Growth:* Take the initiative to find out where you are weak, broken, or immature.

    — Ask God to search you and know you (Psalm 139:23–24).

    — Ask people who know you for their opinions too. Whom will you ask—and when?

- *Find Growth Contexts:* It is our responsibility to research and seek out people and places where spiritual growth occurs.

    — What kind of spiritual growth are you seeking?

    — What might be a good context for such growth—and who can help you locate one?

- **Ask for Reality and Truth:** Take the initiative to get information about your issues from God and others. Be vulnerable to feedback from others.

  — Why is this task important?

  — Who are some safe people in your life, people you can ask for reality and truth? When will you ask one of these for feedback? How do you want to respond?

- **Bring Your Heart to Relationship:** It takes work to keep your heart available and vulnerable. The human tendency is to withhold or protect. Yet the fruit of growth comes when you let others inside (2 Cor. 6:12–13).

  — What realities of your past, what sins, and what hurts do you need to bring into relationship with God and with others?

  — Why haven't you done so? What will you do to overcome those obstacles? Who will support you and/or pray for you as you work to keep your heart vulnerable?

- **Take Risks in Areas That Need Stretching:** This may involve, for instance, being more honest than you are used to, being more open to feeling close when you are not comfortable, or sitting with painful emotions you normally would avoid.

  — What one or two growth areas in your life (maybe one of the three just listed) will involve taking risks? Be specific about the growth and the possible risks.

— What kind of support do you have as you take those risks—or where can you find some support?

FIXING THE PASSIVITY PROBLEM (Page 340)

When people allow life to happen to them or when they react to others rather than taking initiative, they take a passive role. Here are some of the causes of and solutions to such passivity.

- ***Misunderstanding the Bible's Message:*** God addresses passivity as a problem, not a virtue (Matt. 25:14–30). Passivity negates risk and initiative and, ultimately, growth. When we are passive, we shrink from the risks of the faith life itself. Furthermore, activity is bad when it takes the place of relationship rather than serving the purposes of relationship. Activity was designed by God to involve us in the work of life, not to replace closeness.

  — Study the examples of biblical figures who experienced many miracles and encounters with God. What activity, involvement, and work characterized the life of Abraham, David, Mary the mother of Jesus, and/or Peter?

  — God has his job to do, and we have ours. When have you, like the person trying to use willpower to stop a drinking problem, tried to do God's job? What resulted from your efforts?

  — When have you, like the person who waits for someone in his life to become aware that she is being hurtful rather than say something to her, demanded that God do your job? What resulted from your lack of efforts?

— In what current area(s) of your life are you either trying to use willpower to change or waiting for a change to happen almost magically instead of addressing the issue with the person involved? What would be a better path—and what will enable you to get on that path?

• **Fear of Failure:** Some people are passive because they are afraid to fail.

— Are you afraid to fail? What are the roots of that fear—and what fuels it today?

— When has failing at something not been as awful as you had anticipated? What could you have done at the time to make it even more of a friend to you? What positive learning opportunity was thinly veiled by the failure?

— In what area of your life are you being passive because of a fear of failure? What will you do to overcome that fear? Whom will you turn to for support?

• **Rescue Wishes:** Rescue wishes are desires for someone to take care of us. All people have them to a greater or lesser degree.

— In what current situation(s) are you particularly aware of your rescue wishes?

— What would be an active and therefore healthier role for you in each of those?

We hope you are learning the benefits of taking initiative in spiritual growth. But let us warn you that sometimes active people are impatient and want results yesterday! So, in the final chapter, we learn how we need to submit to the process of time in our growth.

Lord God, you know all too well when I tend to be passive, when I'm reluctant to take risks, when I'm just plain lazy. All of these, Lord, suggest my lack of trust in you and my lack of appreciation for the growth opportunities you give me. Forgive me, Lord. Forgive me too, Lord, for the ways I'm not "working out my salvation with fear and trembling" (Phil. 2:12). And please give me the courage to do so. Please keep me humbled (as I'm feeling right now) and show me the areas where I am weak, broken, or immature, areas where I need healing. Help me find places where I can grow and please grant me the courage to ask for and hear the truth about myself as well as a willingness to take risks. Help me be an able partner with you in my own spiritual surgery. I pray in Jesus' name. Amen.

TIPS FOR GROWERS:

- Consider the various ways God actively works for your betterment. Let that model prompt you to take initiative in your own growth process.

- Review times in your life when you were passive or fearful and missed opportunities God intended for you. Investigate the reasons behind this passivity or fear and resolve these issues.

- Be aware of any tendency to see spiritual growth as something only God does. Instead, look at what you can do to partner with God. Deal with any devaluing attitudes toward activity, such as "It's not being spiritual" or "It's not trusting God." Also, let go of any passive rescue wishes you might have. Replace them with the idea that you can partner with God and others.

- In relationships, take initiative in reconciling with people as opposed to waiting on them to approach you, apologize, and so on. Give up fairness in favor of reconciliatory activity.

CHAPTER NINETEEN

Waiting for the Harvest: Time

The most common question I (John) hear from people in spiritual growth is "Why is this taking so long?" Like Robin, they will often enter the growth process with great hope and excitement. Then, somewhere along the way, they become discouraged that they aren't achieving results as soon as they would like. The purpose of this chapter is to look at the role of the process of time as well as steps along the path of spiritual growth.

THE PROCESS OF TIME (Page 347)

Many growers expect that, if they read their Bibles and do the right things, they will instantly and permanently change. They are disappointed when this does not happen. But time is a necessary ingredient of growth.

- When God's wonderful creation was marred by sin, he knew that two things were necessary to fix the problem: an atoning death to satisfy the requirements of his holiness and a process of repair for his creation to be redeemed and healed from what it had brought upon itself. This process we call time. Explain our analogy and its ramifications for eternity: "Time takes the creation out of the eternal state, as quarantine takes a sick person out of the community." (The discussion is found in the second full paragraph on page 348 of the text.)

- Explain also how the gift of time applies in the lives of individuals and therefore what it means to grow in salvation (1 Peter 2:2).

We aren't negating miracles by this discussion of time. The Bible and our own experience show that God does do instant and marvelous things. At the same time, however, the norm taught in the Scriptures is a model for growth (Mark 4:26–29; Eph. 2:20–21; 4:15–16; Col. 2:19; 2 Peter 3:18). So work on the process and be open to the miraculous. God is for us in both ways.

SO WHAT TAKES ALL THE TIME? (Page 349)

Consider now these specific ways in which time is a necessary part of growth.

- **Experience Versus Intellectual Learning:** Spiritual growth involves the whole person. All of our parts need to be exposed to God's love and healing: heart, soul, and mind (Matt. 22:37). This means that growth is much more than cognitively understanding or memorizing a fact, idea, or principle. We need to add experience to our intellectual grasp of growth, and experience, by definition, takes time.

  — When have you realized that understanding something in your head is not the same as knowing wholeness and health?

  — Describe a time, if you can, when you learned from experience a lesson you already knew in your head. Why was the experiential knowledge important?

  — What intellectual understanding of yours has never been backed up by experience? Where is there a vacuum?

- **Taking in Grace and Forgiveness:** Of all the principles of growth, internalizing God's grace and forgiveness takes the most time. It is unnatural for us to live by grace and forgiveness. That which is not natural requires more time.

— What are you doing to try to earn God's love?

— What taste have you had of living by grace and forgiveness? If that concept is foreign to you, where will you go to learn by experience what it is to live by grace and forgiveness?

— To whom in your life can you extend grace and forgiveness and perhaps be used by the Lord to offer a healing touch?

• ***Repeated Exposure to the Elements of Growth:*** Another reason we need time to grow is that it takes more than one "inoculation" for us to mature. A single lesson or experience is not enough. Growth often requires repetition to sink into our heart and character.

— When have you benefited from the repetition of a growth lesson? Be specific about the lesson and the repeated "inoculations."

— Consider some resources for growth you've already encountered and some lessons to which you've already been introduced. In which of these areas would repeated exposure be beneficial to you?

— Which of these reasons why repetition is necessary for growth have you experienced? Describe the situation(s).

We have many parts to our soul, and we work on an issue at deeper levels.

We are often afraid of truth and light, and we will resist it.

Often we are on another path than God's.

Turning our soul around involves trials, risks, and failures.

— With which of these four reasons are you currently wrestling?

- *Internal Versus External Change:* Internal changes of heart and life mean true character growth. As hearts are transformed, they also transform the external life. But this takes time.

    — What external, behavioral change in yourself would you make instantly if you had the power?

    — What internal issue is at the root of the external issue you just identified — or where will you go to figure it out?

    — The woman's weight problem stemmed from her fear of closeness and vulnerability. When she worked on the internal, the external change she had long wanted took place — and lasted. Describe a similar experience that you've had.

Don't ignore a crisis in favor of addressing the internal issues behind that crisis. Rather, deal with both at the same time. Get help with the crisis and keep working on whatever soul issue is driving the struggle.

DETERMINING LENGTH OF THE GROWTH PROCESS
(Page 352)

As we deal with the most commonly asked question—"Why is this taking so long?"—we encounter what is probably the second-most-often-asked question: "How can I know how long it will all take?"

- The growth process generally takes more time than you thought.
    — What is freeing about the fact that, for God, normal life is being in the growth process for life?

    — When have you experienced the truth that "issues and struggles may and should change over time, but growth is not a season"?

That said, let me explain that several indicators can give a sense of how long specific growth or repair issues take to resolve. Put together, these indicators can help you get a sense of time for your work.

- Review the four indicators listed below.

    Severity of the issue. Generally speaking, the worse the issue, the longer the time required to resolve it.

    Onset of the issue. Generally, the earlier the problem, the more time it will take to deal successfully with it.

    Available resources. Although the work of spiritual growth is, at its heart, a miraculous act of God, it still requires resources, such as a healthy support system, a balanced church, good materials to study, appropriate leadership, and frequent meetings. The more resources available, the less time is needed.

    Spiritual poverty. People who are truly aware of their need and hunger for God and growth will go and get it. They will unveil their souls, expose their weaknesses, accept comfort and correction, and try their mightiest to grow in God's ways. And they will grow and resolve issues!

— What impact has one or more of these factors had on your growth process? Explain.

— What do these indicators suggest about how long you'll be working on the issue that is the most pressing to you at the moment?

— The last two indicators are things with which you can be proactive. What will you do about them?

THE PLACE OF THE PAST (Page 354)

Time is also important in the role the past plays in our growth. Here are some key principles.

- ***An Unresolved Issue May Mean That Part of a Person's Soul Is Still "in the Past":*** When a person struggles, he experiences some aspect of himself as split off and lost in an injured or unloved state. It is as if the person grew up on the outside but left a part of himself behind, still alone or attacked or overwhelmed.

    — What aspect(s) of yourself do you currently experience as split off and lost in an injured or unloved state?

    — When have you brought into the present for healing and growth a part of you still in the past? Describe both that part of you and the healing you received.

— Where can or will you go to find the resources so that this immature or wounded aspect of you can mature and repair and be integrated into the present?

- **Most Spiritual, Emotional, and Relational Issues Have a History:** Struggles don't come from out of the blue. Our problems, issues, and doubts all have roots in the past. Often understanding a pattern will help a person grow.

  — What pattern from your past has contributed to an area of struggle involving parenting, guilt, faith doubts, passivity, or something else?

  — To whom might you go for help seeing a pattern in your life that you may not be seeing?

- **Forgiveness Requires a Past:** Understanding your past both factually and emotionally is key to forgiving. After all, if the past is not relevant, there is nothing either to forgive or to be forgiven for.

  — Why is factual understanding of your past insufficient? Put differently, why must we understand our past both factually and emotionally?

  — Give an example (ideally from your own life) of how understanding the past has been key to extending or receiving forgiveness.

- *Trauma:* Often, as people feel safe in a growth context, their past will come back to them with a vengeance. The safety of love, grace, and structure makes it possible for them to bear what was previously unbearable. When have you experienced your past coming back to you with a vengeance? Describe the safety you had finally found as the old hurts, feelings, memories, or terrors resurfaced.

THE PATH OF GROWTH (Page 357)

God uses the passage of time as one element of growth for his people. Within time, growth follows a defined order that shows that spiritual movement is occurring. Since God wants you to be a co-laborer in this process (Phil. 2:12–13), let's look at the essential aspects of this path so you know what to expect.

- *Need, or Bad Fruit:* The process of spiritual growth begins in most people with either a recognized need for God or growth, or some struggle or problem for which they need God's help. These struggles begin the process because they indicate that we do not possess all we need.

  — What started you down the path of spiritual growth? What circumstances, for instance, helped you realize that you do not possess all you need?

  — Read through the following list of "fruit struggles," the types that people might bring into a growth setting that are actually the fruit of deeper spiritual issues. Which one(s) are you dealing with now?

  Marriage or dating conflicts

  Depression

  Doubt

  Addictions

  Family problems

  Anxiety

  Career failures

  Troublesome emotions

  Hurts from the past

— What deeper spiritual issues do you think underlie the issues you just identified? What steps could you take to identify those issues?

- **A Relational Arena for Growth:** Spiritual growth doesn't occur in a vacuum. It happens within intimate, vulnerable relationships with God and safe people (Eccl. 4:9–12).

 — Who is a safe person for you? If your list is short or nonexistent, where might you go to find supportive and safe friends?

 — For whom are you or could you be a safe person?

- **Identification of Issues:** Character injuries and immaturities are the central issues that drive the fruit, or symptoms. Realize that different issues can drive the same symptom.

 — Which of these issues are you dealing with—or have you had to address in the past?

 Lack of bonding and trust

 Problems being separate and setting limits

 Problems controlling others

 Inability to deal with your badness

 Problems accepting the failures of others

 Struggles in relating to the world as an adult

— Where can you go or with whom can you talk in order to get help identifying the issue underneath what is going on in your life?

- *Ownership:* As people become educated about their particular issues, they will need to take responsibility for them. Understanding the past helps them see what parts are their fault, what parts are others' fault, and what parts are the product of living in a fallen world. Ownership means that the person comes to the realization that her life is her problem and that her growth is the solution.

  — Think about what you've learned about your past. What issues that you're dealing with are your fault (denial, rescuing, fear of loss), what parts are others' fault (control, withholding of love, nonacceptance), and what parts are the product of living in a fallen world (death of a loved one, a chronic illness)?

  — Why do you hesitate to take ownership of your life? Why is such ownership fundamental to growth?

- *Rebuilding Tasks:* Here people begin using the love, support, and structure of others to develop what they do not possess inside. Exercising, risk, and practice with injured parts within safe relationships help people grow.

  — What "exercise" are you currently doing to strengthen or develop new relationship muscles?

  — What risk would you like to be able to take—and what is holding you back? What can you do to move forward?

- ***Forgiveness and Grief:*** At some point, having owned the issues, people need to let go of debts, feel sadness about the past and losses they can't change, and receive forgiveness for what they have contributed.

  — Are you at this point? More specifically, do you own the issue(s) calling for forgiveness and grief? Explain why you've answered yes or no.

  — What debts do you need to let go of? What events or losses from the past do you need to let yourself feel sadness about? And for what do you need to receive God's forgiveness?

- ***Good Fruit:*** As the inside grows, so ultimately should the outside. You should see better relationships, more fulfilling emotional experiences such as gratitude and joy, and greater connectedness to God. What evidence of growth, what signs of this good fruit, have you noticed? You might ask a trusted friend who has known you for a while to help you answer this question. That person might have a better perspective on your own growth.

- ***Deepening:*** Growth never ends on this earth. People will find new areas of growth as God helps them search their hearts (Ps. 139:23–24). When have you experienced the end of a crisis as actually the beginning of the real work of growth? Describe the situation and the growth that has resulted and may even be continuing.

Wise individuals who are committed to growth will look long and hard at the person in the mirror (James 1:23–25) and go deeper inside their soul, bringing more and more to the light of God's healing grace.

Lord God, forgive me for my impatience with the growth process you've designed, for my arrogant thinking that a speedier path would be better, and for my prideful desire that life goes according to my timetable. Lord, please guide me on this path of growth, showing me any part of my soul that may still be "in the past." Teach me to take ownership of my issues, give me courage to do the rebuilding tasks ahead, and enable me to persevere as I both wait for the good fruit and tackle deeper issues. Most important, in all this, Lord, may you be glorified as you do your work in me and through me. I pray in Jesus' name. Amen.

TIPS FOR GROWERS:

- Change your mind-set from an instant-results mentality to an acceptance of the fact that the biblical process of growth bears fruit over time. Understand both why growth takes time and the purpose of time in that process.

- Confess and repent of any performance-based, perfectionistic, or grandiose tendencies to be in control of the time your growth requires.

- Use time to your advantage by being willing to expose yourself repeatedly to the same growth experiences until you internalize them.

For information on books, resources, or speaking engagements:

Cloud-Townsend Resources
3176 Pullman Avenue, Suite 104
Costa Mesa, CA 92626
Phone: 1-800-676-HOPE (4673)
Web: www.cloudtownsend.com

Understanding the Biblical Process of Growth to
Help People Move into Christ-like Maturity

HOW PEOPLE GROW
What the Bible Reveals about Personal Growth
Dr. Henry Cloud and Dr. John Townsend

Does Christianity really work? Why do many sincere Christians fail to make progress in some area of their lives even though they work hard to apply the spiritual solutions they have been taught? They learn about God's love, yet continue to feel depressed. They understand the crucified life, but still struggle with problems in their relationships. They focus on their security in Christ, but continue to overeat. "Spiritual interventions" are not working for them.

To solve this dilemma, authors Henry Cloud and John Townsend examined the processes and paths that actually help people grow and made a discovery. They went to the Bible and found that the true processes that make people grow are all there. Not only is the Bible true, but what is true is in the Bible. The problem, they contend, is that many systems of growth leave out much of what the Bible teaches.

In this foundational work, Cloud and Townsend describe the principles they use in their private practice, in their teaching and seminars, and in their writing of books like *Boundaries, Changes That Heal,* and *Safe People.* Their practical approach to helping people grow really works and has such transforming power in people's lives because their principles are grounded in both orthodox Christian faith and a keen understanding of human nature. This book will be useful both to those who are helping people grow spiritually, as well as to those who are seeking growth themselves.

Hardcover 0-310-22153-6
Abridged Audio Pages® Cassette 0-310-24065-4
Workbook 0-310-24569-9

ZONDERVAN™

GRAND RAPIDS, MICHIGAN 49530 USA

WWW.ZONDERVAN.COM

Best-Selling *Boundaries* books available from
Dr. Henry Cloud and Dr. John Townsend

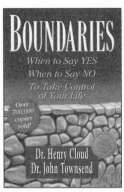

BOUNDARIES

Presents a biblical treatment of boundaries, identifies how bound-aries are developed and how they become injured, shows Christian misconceptions of their function and purpose, and gives a program for developing and maintaining healthy limits.

Over 700,000 copies sold!

Hardcover 0-310-58590-2
Softcover 0-310-24745-4
Abridged Audio Pages® Cassette 0-310-58598-8
Unabridged Audio Pages® Cassette 0-310-24331-9
Unabridged Audio Pages® CD 0-310-24180-4
Workbook 0-310-49481-8
Zondervan*Groupware*™ 0-310-22362-8
Leader's Guide 0-310-22452-7
Participant's Guide 0-310-22453-5

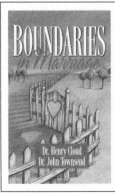

BOUNDARIES IN MARRIAGE

Helps you understand the friction points or serious hurts and be-trayals in your marriage—and move beyond them to the mutual care, respect, affirmation, and intimacy you both long for.

Hardcover 0-310-22151-X
Softcover 0-310-24314-9
Abridged Audio Pages® Cassette 0-310-22549-3
Unabridged Audio Pages® Cassette 0-310-23849-8
Workbook 0-310-22875-1
Zondervan*Groupware*™ 0-310-24612-1
Leader's Guide 0-310-24614-8
Participant's Guide 0-31-24615-6

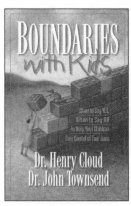

BOUNDARIES WITH KIDS

Helps parents set boundaries with their children and helps them teach their children the concept of boundaries.

Hardcover 0-310-20035-0
Softcover 0-310-24315-7
Abridged Audio Pages® Cassette 0-310-20456-9
Workbook 0-310-22349-0

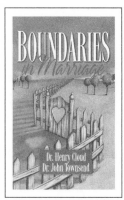

BOUNDARIES IN DATING

Road map to the kind of enjoyable, rewarding dating that can take you from weekends alone to a lifetime with the soul mate you've longed for.

Softcover 0-310-20034-2
Abridged Audio Pages® Cassette 0-310-24055-0
Workbook 0-310-23330-5
Zondervan*Groupware*™ 0-310-23873-0
Leader's Guide 0-310-23874-9
Participant's Guide 0-310-23875-7

Pick up a copy today at your favorite bookstore!

ZONDERVAN™

GRAND RAPIDS, MICHIGAN 49530 USA

WWW.ZONDERVAN.COM

Other Great Books by Dr. Henry Cloud and Dr. John Townsend

RAISING GREAT KIDS
A Comprehensive Guide to Parenting with Grace and Truth

Hardcover 0-310-22569-8
Softcover 0-310-23549-9
Abridged Audio Pages® Cassette 0-310-22572-8
Workbook for Parents of Preschoolers 0-310-22571-X
Workbook for Parents of School-Age Children 0-310-23452-2
Workbook for Parents of Teenagers 0-310-23437-9
Zondervan*Groupware*™ for
  Parents of Preschoolers 0-310-23238-4
  Parents of Preschoolers Leader's Guide 0-310-23296-1
  Parents of Preschoolers Participant's Guide 0-310-23295-3

SAFE PEOPLE
How to Find Relationships That Are Good for You and Avoid Those That Aren't

Softcover 0-310-21084-4
Mass Market 0-310-49501-6

CHANGES THAT HEAL
How to Understand Your Past to Ensure a Healthier Future
Dr. Henry Cloud

Softcover 0-310-60631-4
Mass Market 0-310-21463-7
Audio Pages® Abridged Cassette 0-310-20567-0
Workbook 0-310-60633-0

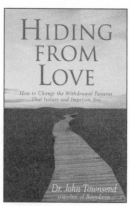

HIDING FROM LOVE
How to Change the Withdrawal Patterns That Isolate and Imprison You

Dr. John Townsend

Softcover 0-310-20107-1
Workbook 0-310-23828-5

THE MOM FACTOR
Identifies six types of moms and shows how they profoundly affect our lives.

Softcover 0-310-22559-0

Pick up a copy today at your favorite bookstore!

ZONDERVAN™

GRAND RAPIDS, MICHIGAN 49530 USA

WWW.ZONDERVAN.COM

We want to hear from you. Please send your comments about this book to us in care of the address below. Thank you.

GRAND RAPIDS, MICHIGAN 49530 USA

WWW.ZONDERVAN.COM